COUNTRIES, REGIONAL STUDIES, TRADING BLOCKS, UNIONS, WORLD ORGANIZATIONS



# CHILE

# CONDITIONS, ISSUES AND U.S. RELATIONS

# COUNTRIES, REGIONAL STUDIES, TRADING BLOCKS, UNIONS, WORLD ORGANIZATIONS

Additional books in this series can be found on Nova's website under the Series tab.

Additional e-books in this series can be found on Nova's website under the e-book tab.

COUNTRIES, REGIONAL STUDIES, TRADING BLOCKS, UNIONS, WORLD ORGANIZATIONS

# CHILE

# CONDITIONS, ISSUES AND U.S. RELATIONS

GARRETT M. ULRICH
EDITOR

NOVINKA

*New York*

For permission to use material from this book please contact us:
Telephone 631-231-7269; Fax 631-231-8175
Web Site: http://www.novapublishers.com



**Library of Congress Cataloging-in-Publication Data**

ISBN: 978-1-61122-031-5

*Published by Nova Science Publishers, Inc. † New York*

# CONTENTS

| | | |
|---|---|---|
| **Preface** | | **vii** |
| **Chapter 1** | Chile: Political and Economic Conditions and U.S. Relations<br>*Peter J. Meyer* | **1** |
| **Chapter 2** | Chile's Pension System: Background in Brief<br>*Alison M. Shelton* | **27** |
| **Chapter 3** | Chile 2013 Human Rights Report<br>*U.S. Department of State; Bureau of Democracy, Human Rights and Labor* | **41** |
| **Chapter 4** | Chile 2012 International Religious Freedom Report<br>*U.S. Department of State; Bureau of Democracy, Human Rights and Labor* | **71** |
| **Chapter 5** | 2013 Investment Climate Statement: Chile<br>*Bureau of Economic and Business Affairs* | **77** |
| **Index** | | **101** |

# PREFACE

Located in the Southern Cone of South America, Chile is a politically stable, upper-middle-income, developing nation of 17.5 million people. Chile has maintained friendly relations with the United States since its transition back to civilian democratic rule in 1990. The Obama Administration has sought to build on these traditionally close ties and encourage Chile's leadership in the Western Hemisphere. Bilateral commercial relations are particularly strong; total trade in goods and services has more than tripled since the implementation of a free trade agreement in 2004. Additional areas of cooperation include supporting regional stability and promoting clean energy development. This book discusses the political and economic conditions of Chile, as well as their relations with the United States. It also discusses Chile's public pension system, which consists of three tiers that include a poverty prevention tier, an individual account tier, and a voluntary savings tier. The book concludes with the Chile 2013 human right report, the 2012 international religious freedom report, and the 2013 invest climate statement.

Chapter 1 – Chile has maintained friendly relations with the United States since its transition back to civilian democratic rule in 1990. The Obama Administration has sought to build on these traditionally close ties and encourage Chile's leadership in the Western Hemisphere. Bilateral commercial relations are particularly strong; total trade in goods and services has more than tripled since the implementation of a free trade agreement in 2004. Additional areas of cooperation include supporting regional stability and promoting clean energy development.

Chapter 2 – In 1980, Chile was the first country to replace its pay-as-you-go public pension system with a system of individual accounts. The "Chilean model" has been widely studied as one possible model for public pension restructuring. Chile's public pension system consists of three tiers: a poverty prevention tier, an individual account tier, and a voluntary savings tier. The poverty prevention tier provides a minimum benefit to aged persons who did not participate in the public pension system and to retired workers whose monthly pensions financed by individual account assets (the second tier) do not reach certain thresholds. Workers contribute 10% of wage or salary income to an individual account in the second tier and choose a private-sector Administradora de Fondos de Pensiones (AFP) with which to invest their pension contributions. Employers are not required to contribute to employees' AFPs, although since 2008 employers have been required to pay the premiums for workers' survivor and disability insurance, which are provided by private insurance companies. Upon retirement, the worker may withdraw assets that have accumulated in the individual account as an immediate or deferred annuity or through programmed withdrawals. The third tier allows workers to supplement retirement income with voluntary, tax-favored savings. In 2008, Chile approved major reforms intended, among other goals, to increase participation in the public pension system, improve competition among the private-sector individual account managers, and bolster the poverty prevention tier. There has been concern that, as a result of low participation rates and underreporting, many workers could reach retirement with individual account balances that are too small to provide an adequate pension annuity. The 2008 reforms helped address these concerns by expanding the poverty prevention tier, phasing in coverage for most self-employed workers, and providing incentives for additional voluntary saving through the system's third tier. Other provisions approved in 2008 are intended to reduce high investment management fees (administrative costs) by increasing competition among AFPs.

Chapter 3 – Chile is a constitutional multi-party democracy. On December 15, in a presidential run-off following congressional, regional council, and a first round of presidential elections on November 17, Chileans elected former president Michelle Bachelet as their next president. All of the elections were considered to be free and fair. The new government will take office in March 2014. Authorities generally maintained effective control over the security forces. Security forces occasionally committed human rights abuses. The principal human rights problems concerned discrimination against indigenous populations; societal violence and discrimination against women, children, and lesbian, gay, bisexual, and transgender (LGBT) persons; child labor; and harsh prison conditions and treatment. Additional human rights concerns in the country included use of excessive force and abuse by security forces, isolated reports of government corruption, and anti-Semitism. The government generally took steps to prosecute officials who committed abuses. Nevertheless, many human rights organizations contended that security officials accused of committing abuses have impunity.

Chapter 4 – The constitution and other laws and policies protect religious freedom and, in practice, the government generally respected religious freedom. The trend in the government's respect for religious freedom did not change significantly during the year. There were reports of societal abuses or discrimination based on religious affiliation, belief, or practice. Incidents of anti-Semitism included online harassment, verbal slurs, and increased vandalism. U.S. embassy officials discussed religious tolerance with the National Office of Religious Affairs (ONAR) and leaders of numerous religious groups, focusing on the value of deepening institutional cooperation. The embassy organized an iftar with an ecumenical group of religious leaders, and embassy officers attended interfaith events.

Chapter 5 – For the last three decades, Chile has made foreign direct investment (FDI) an essential part of its national development strategy. Chile's sound, market-oriented policies have created significant opportunities for foreign investors to participate in the country's steady economic growth. Chile's business climate is generally straightforward and transparent. Foreign investors receive treatment similar to Chilean nationals in nearly all sectors. There are generally no special exemptions or incentives for FDI as a matter of policy. A broad political consensus on the advantages of foreign investment means that Chile's policies towards FDI are unlikely to change.

In: Chile
Editor: Garrett M. Ulrich

ISBN: 978-1-61122-031-5


*Chapter 1*

# CHILE: POLITICAL AND ECONOMIC CONDITIONS AND U.S. RELATIONS*

***Peter J. Meyer***

## SUMMARY

Chile has maintained friendly relations with the United States since its transition back to civilian democratic rule in 1990. The Obama Administration has sought to build on these traditionally close ties and encourage Chile's leadership in the Western Hemisphere. Bilateral commercial relations are particularly strong; total trade in goods and services has more than tripled since the implementation of a free trade agreement in 2004. Additional areas of cooperation include supporting regional stability and promoting clean energy development.

## Political Situation

Sebastián Piñera of the center-right "Alliance for Chile" is now in the final months of his four-year presidential term. Lacking majorities in both houses of the Chilean Congress, Piñera has had to secure the support of opposition or

---

* This is an edited, reformatted and augmented version of Congressional Research Service Publication, No. R40126, dated January 10, 2014.

unaffiliated legislators to advance his business-friendly agenda. While he has won legislative support for a variety of incremental policy reforms, Piñera has struggled to deal with a series of popular protests over issues ranging from energy policy to the education system. Analysts maintain that the Chilean populace has resorted to such tactics to demonstrate its dissatisfaction with the country's political class, which it views as unresponsive to citizen demands and unwilling to address high levels of inequality. Former President Michelle Bachelet (2006-2010) was elected to a new four-year presidential term in December 2013 and is scheduled to take office on March 11, 2014. Her center-left "New Majority" coalition also won majorities in both houses of the Chilean Congress after campaigning on a platform promising significant education, fiscal, and constitutional reforms designed to reduce inequality and improve social mobility. Bachelet may face some challenges holding her ideologically diverse coalition together, but she should be able to enact much of her policy agenda. Education and constitutional reforms, however, require congressional supermajorities and will require Bachelet to win support from unaffiliated and opposition legislators.

## Economic Conditions

According to many analysts, Chile has the most competitive and fundamentally sound economy in Latin America. Chile's economic success stems from policies implemented over several decades that have opened the country to investment, secured access to foreign markets, and mitigated the effects of external shocks. In recent years, this solid policy framework has helped the Chilean economy weather the global financial crisis and a massive February 2010 earthquake. Strong economic growth—paired with targeted social assistance programs—has also contributed to a significant decline in the poverty rate. High levels of inequality have persisted, however, contributing to some popular discontent with Chile's generally strong economic performance.

## Congressional Action

Congress has expressed interest in a variety of issues in U.S.-Chilean relations over the years. The 113$^{th}$ Congress could take up matters such as the U.S.-Chile bilateral income tax treaty, which was signed in 2010 and was submitted to the U.S. Senate for ratification on May 17, 2012 (Treaty Doc.

112-8). Ongoing negotiations over the proposed Trans-Pacific Partnership (TPP) trade agreement, which includes Chile, the United States, and at least 10 other nations in the Asia-Pacific region, may also attract congressional attention.

## Political and Economic Background

Located in the Southern Cone of South America, Chile is a politically stable, uppermiddle-income, developing nation of 17.5 million people.[1] The country declared independence from Spain in 1810 but did not achieve full independence until 1818. By 1932, Chile had established a mass electoral democracy, which endured until 1973. During much of this period, Chile was governed by presidents who pursued state-led development and the social and political incorporation of the working classes. These policies were expanded following the election of Eduardo Frei Montalva of the Christian Democratic Party (*Partido Demócrata Cristiana*, PDC) in 1964. Frei's reformist government took majority ownership of the copper mines, redistributed land, and improved access to education. Despite these actions, some Chileans felt more radical policies were needed.

**Chile in Brief**

**Land Area:** 287,000 square miles
(approximately twice as large as Montana)
**Population:** 17.5 million (2012)
**Ethnic Groups:** 89.7% White or *Mestizo*
(White-Indigenous); 10.3% Indigenous (2012)
**Religion:** 67.4% Roman Catholic; 16.6% Evangelical;
11.6% none (2012)
**Official Language:** Spanish
**Life Expectancy:** 79 years (2011)
**Infant Mortality Rate:** 8 per 100,000 live births (2012)
**Adult Literacy Rate:** 97.8% (2012) Poverty Rate: 14.4% (2011)
**GDP:** $268.2 billion (2012)
**GDP per Capita:** $15,410 (2012)

Sources: Chilean Ministry of Social Development, Chilean National Statistics Institute, International Monetary Fund, World Bank.

In 1970, Salvador Allende, a Socialist and the leader of the leftist "Popular Unity" (*Unidad Popular*) coalition, was elected president in a three-way race with slightly over 36% of the vote. Allende accelerated and furthered the changes of the previous administration by fully nationalizing firms, expanding land reform, and generally socializing the economy. While Allende's supporters pushed him to move more quickly, the political center, represented by the PDC, joined with the parties of the right to block Popular Unity initiatives in the legislature. This ideological intransigence prevented the Chilean government from addressing the faltering economy and served to further radicalize supporters on both ends of Chile's already polarized society. When the situation continued to deteriorate following indecisive 1973 legislative elections, the military intervened.[2]

## Pinochet Era

On September 11, 1973, the Chilean military, under the control of General Augusto Pinochet, deposed the Allende government in a violent coup and quickly consolidated control of the country. The military junta closed Congress, censored the media, declared political parties in recess, and regarded the organized left as an internal enemy of the state. Within the first few months of military rule, over 1,800 people in Chile were killed or "disappeared" for political reasons, and some 23,000 were imprisoned or tortured. By the end of the dictatorship in 1990, the number of killed or disappeared had risen to at least 3,216 and the number of imprisoned and tortured exceeded 38,000.[3]

General Pinochet emerged as the figurehead of the junta soon after the coup and won a tightly controlled referendum to institutionalize his regime in 1978. Pinochet reversed decades of statist economic policies by rapidly implementing a series of changes that liberalized trade and investment, privatized firms, and dismantled the welfare state. He won another tightly controlled referendum in 1980, which approved the constitution that continues to govern Chile today.

The new constitution called for a plebiscite to take place in 1988 in which Chileans would have the opportunity to reelect Pinochet to another eight-year term or reject him in favor of contested elections. Although the Chilean economy enjoyed a period of rapid economic growth between 1976 and 1981, a banking crisis from 1981 to 1984 sparked widespread protests. Following these initial demonstrations, Chilean civil society groups became more active in criticizing the policies of the Pinochet regime. At the same time, political parties began to reemerge to challenge the government. In 1988, several civil society groups and political parties formed a coalition in opposition to Pinochet's reelection.

In the plebiscite, 55% of the Chilean people voted against another eight-year term for Pinochet, triggering the election campaign of 1989.[4]

## Return to Democracy and the *Concertación* Era

Two major coalitions of parties contested the elections of 1989. The center-left "Coalition of Parties for Democracy," (*Concertación de Partidos por la Democracia*, Concertación) united parties opposed to the Pinochet dictatorship, including the centrist PDC and the center-left Party for Democracy (*Partido por la Democracia*, PPD). The center-right "Democracy and Progress" (*Democracia y Progreso*) coalition included the center-right National Renewal (*Renovación Nacional*, RN) and the rightist Independent Democratic Union (*Unión Demócrata Independiente*, UDI). Patricio Aylwin, a Christian Democrat and the candidate of the Concertación, won the presidency with 55% of the vote and the Concertación won majorities in the Chamber of Deputies and among the elected members of the Senate.

Presidents from the Concertación governed Chile for 20 consecutive years following the return of democracy to the country. President Aylwin (1990-1994) was followed by Eduardo Frei RuizTagle of the PDC (1994-2000), Ricardo Lagos of both the Socialist Party (*Partido Socalista,* PS) and the PPD (2000-2006), and Michelle Bachelet of the PS (2006-2010). All four of the Concertación administrations faced significant constraints in governance, however, as a result of undemocratic provisions in the Pinochet-era constitution.

The country's binomial electoral system, composed of two-member districts that require a coalition to win by two-to-one margins in order to secure both seats, led to the significant overrepresentation of the Chilean right in both houses of Congress. Likewise, prior to 2005, nine unelected senators were designated by the military and other government bodies, effectively creating a right-leaning majority in the Senate despite Concertación victories in legislative elections.

Moreover, the Chilean military maintained a powerful, independent role following the democratic transition, and Pinochet remained the head of the army until 1998 and then served as a lifetime senator until 2002. These authoritarian institutional features forced the Concertación to govern through pacts with the Chilean right, greatly inhibiting the pace of policy changes.[5]

Despite these challenges, the Concertación was able to implement gradual economic, social, and political reforms while in power. Although the Concertación administrations largely maintained the market-oriented economic framework they inherited, they also made a number of changes. Whereas Pinochet unilaterally reduced tariffs, the Concertación governments negotiated a broad network of free trade agreements to obtain reciprocal access to important consumer markets and fuel export-led development. The Concertación also institutionalized countercyclical fiscal policies to ensure stable government funding during economic downturns, and built a modest social safety net.[6] During two decades of Concertación rule, Chile's economy grew by an average of 5.1% annually, and the percentage of Chileans living in poverty fell from 38.8% to 15.1%.[7] Major political reforms were delayed until 2005, when the Concertación won approval for a package of 58 constitutional amendments. The changes included the elimination of unelected and lifetime senators and the establishment of firm civilian control over the military.[8] The Chilean right successfully protected the binomial electoral system, however, which remains in place today.

Efforts to address dictatorship-era human rights abuses were similarly delayed. Although President Aylwin created a National Commission for Truth and Reconciliation (the Rettig Commission) to investigate political disappearances and killings during the authoritarian period, other human rights initiatives advanced slowly. In 2003, President Lagos established a National Commission on Political Imprisonment and Torture (the Valech Commission), which awarded reparations.

During the administration of President Bachelet—who was imprisoned and tortured by the Pinochet regime—Chile created an Institute of Human Rights, ratified the International Convention for the Protection of all Persons from Enforced Disappearance, and established a Museum of Memory dedicated to the victims of the dictatorship and those who struggled to promote and defend human rights. Over time, the Chilean judiciary gradually shifted its jurisprudence on dictatorship-era human rights abuses, ruling the country's 1978 amnesty law inapplicable in some cases.[9] At least 262 individuals have been convicted for human rights violations and more than 1,100 judicial proceedings remain open.[10]

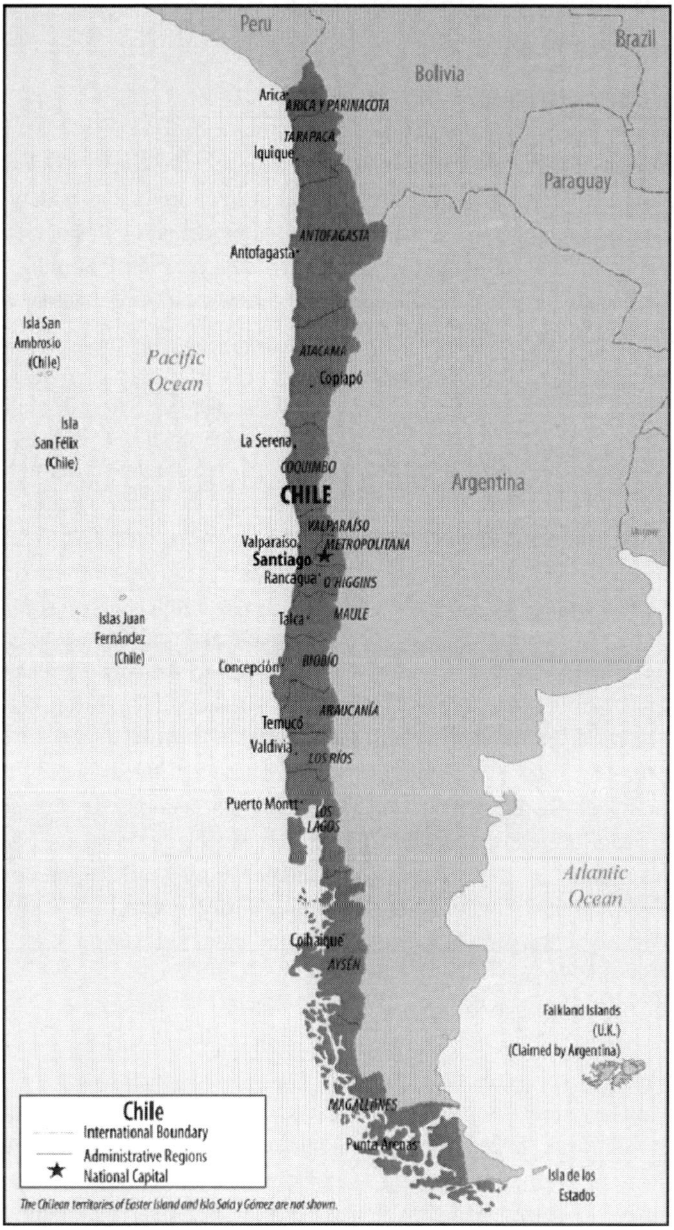


Source: Map Resources, adapted by CRS Graphics.

Figure 1. Map of Chile.

# POLITICAL SITUATION

## Piñera Administration

Sebastián Piñera of the center-right "Alliance for Chile," (*Alianza por Chile*, Alianza)[11] coalition is nearing the end of his four-year presidential term that began in March 2010. He took office after defeating former President Eduardo Frei (1994-2000) of the center-left Concertación coalition, 52% to 48% in a second round runoff election.[12] Piñera's electoral victory was the first for the Chilean right since 1958, and brought an end to 20 years of governance by the Concertación.

Piñera has had to secure the support of unaffiliated and opposition Members of Congress to pass legislation since his coalition does not hold a majority of seats in either house of the Chilean legislature. Although Piñera has successfully implemented portions of his pro-business agenda, such as reducing the number of days it takes to start a business from 27 to 7,[13] several of his legislative compromises have sparked intra-coalition divisions. Conservative sectors of Piñera's coalition, for example, have criticized the administration's willingness to increase taxes and expand social welfare programs. Piñera enacted a temporary tax increase on corporations to help fund reconstruction after a massive February 2010 earthquake, and then made the tax increase permanent as part of a fiscal reform designed to increase funding for education. Piñera has also enacted a new "Ethical Family Income" program, which increases cash subsidies and job training for the poor and expands benefits to low-income Chileans above the poverty line. Although initiatives such as these have consolidated and built upon programs implemented by the Concertación, the opposition has been divided between centrist sectors willing to work with Piñera and more left-leaning sectors intent on opposing his agenda.

In addition to negotiating legislation with the Chilean Congress, Piñera has spent much of his time in office responding to a series of large-scale citizen demonstrations about a variety of social demands, including education, environmental protection, and political decentralization. According to many analysts, Chileans have resorted to street protests as a result of their dissatisfaction with the country's political class, which they view as unresponsive to citizen demands and unwilling to address the country's high level of inequality.[14] This is somewhat counterintuitive since Chile's democracy is more consolidated and inclusive than ever before; elections and respect for individual rights have become normalized, many of the undemocratic provisions of the constitution have been eliminated, and poverty has fallen considerably.[15]

Chileans are also more aware of their rights as a result of these advances, however, and young Chileans—who have no memory of the dictatorship—are much more willing to vocalize their demands.[16] Many are disillusioned with the country's lack of social mobility, and believe that the country's economic gains have not translated into better living conditions and public services for most Chileans.[17]

Since the country's binomial electoral system effectively ensures a relatively equal distribution of power between the two major political coalitions regardless of voters' preferences,[18] elections are extremely limited in their ability to channel citizen discontent. Likewise, candidates have traditionally been chosen through negotiations among political party leaders rather than through primary elections, and political power is heavily concentrated in the central government. Given these constraints on electoral democracy, demonstrations may serve as an alternative mechanism for holding political leaders accountable and forcing them to respond to citizen demands.

While many analysts maintain that the protests and citizen dissatisfaction are unlikely to seriously threaten Chile's political stability in the near term, some argue that socio-economic and political reforms could help ease tensions moving forward.[19] Piñera and the Chilean Congress appear to agree, as they have reacted to the protests by adopting legislation designed to address some of the demonstrators' demands. As noted above, the Chilean government recently adopted a fiscal reform that will allow it to dedicate increased funding to education. Although the changes do not fully address the demands of the protesting students, they will likely make education more affordable for low- and middle-income Chileans. The Chilean government has also adopted electoral reforms to institutionalize primary elections and make it easier to vote.[20] These initiatives have not yet translated into increased support for Chile's political class, however, as just 21% of Chileans approved of the ruling Alianza coalition and 32% approved of the opposition in December 2013.[21]

## 2013 General Elections

On December 15, 2013, former President Michelle Bachelet (2006-2010) won a new four-year term as President of Chile. Representing the center-left "New Majority" (*Nueva Mayoría*) coalition—an electoral pact between the four parties of the former Concertación, the Communist Party (*Partido*

*Comunista*, PC), and a few other small parties, Bachelet easily defeated the ruling Alianza coalition's candidate, Evelyn Matthei, 62%-38% in a second round runoff election.[22]

Bachelet was also the leading vote-getter in the first round election held on November 17, 2013, but was forced into a runoff after failing to secure a majority. She won 47% of the first round vote, and was followed by Matthei (25%), Marco Enriquez-Ominami of the center-left Progressive Party (11%), Franco Parisi, a center-right independent (10%), and five other candidates (7% combined).[23] President Piñera was ineligible to run for reelection since Chile's constitution only allows for nonconsecutive terms.

In legislative elections held concurrently with the first round presidential vote, Bachelet's Nueva Mayoría coalition picked up seats in both houses of the Chilean Congress. It will now hold 67 of 120 seats in the Chamber of Deputies and 21 of 38 seats in the Chilean Senate.[24] Piñera's Alianza coalition will hold 49 seats in the Chamber and 15 seats in the Senate, and legislators unaffiliated with either of the two major coalitions will hold 4 seats in the Chamber and 2 seats in the Senate.[25]

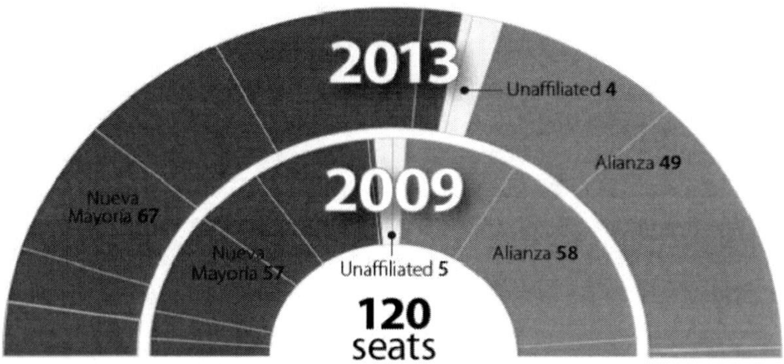


| | Nueva Mayoría | | | | | | Unaffiliated | | | Alianza | | |
|---|---|---|---|---|---|---|---|---|---|---|---|---|
| | PC | PRSD | PPD | PS | PDC | Ind | PRI | PL | Ind | RN | UDI | Ind |
| **2013** | 6 | 6 | 15 | 15 | 21 | 4 | 0 | 1 | 3 | 19 | 29 | 1 |
| **2009** | 3 | 5 | 18 | 11 | 19 | 1 | 3 | 0 | 2 | 18 | 37 | 3 |

Source: Prepared by Amber Hope Wilhelm, CRS Graphics Specialist.

Notes: Several deputies have left the RN since the election. They intend to create a new, more centrist party within the Alianza. See Table A-1 for political party acronyms.

Figure 2. Coalition and Party Affiliation in the Chilean Chamber of Deputies. Seat distribution resulting from the 2009 and 2013 elections.

### *President-elect Bachelet's Policy Proposals*

Throughout her campaign, Bachelet sought to address Chileans' rising expectations, promising to reduce inequality, promote social mobility, and improve public services. The three principal pillars of her platform were education reform, fiscal reform, and constitutional reform. Student demonstrations over the past several years have been the largest and most consistent expression of citizen discontent in Chile. Bachelet has promised to meet several of the protesters' demands, including cutting off government funding to for-profit educational institutions, forbidding primary and secondary schools that receive government funding from selectively admitting students, and guaranteeing free post-secondary education for students from families whose incomes are in the bottom 70% with the intention of providing free tuition for all students within six years.

In order to provide a sustainable source of funding for her education reform, Bachelet has proposed increasing government revenues by 3% of gross domestic product (GDP) over four years. The majority of the new revenues would come from increasing the corporate tax rate from 20% to 25%. The fiscal reform also includes measures to reduce tax evasion, tax incentives for investment and small- and medium-sized enterprises, and a reduction in the top individual tax rate from 40% to 35%. In addition to funding the education reform, the new revenues would be used to strengthen public health, pension, and social protection programs and ensure the government budget is structurally balanced.

Bachelet argues that in order to bring these and other structural changes to fruition, Chile must change its politics. Central to this effort is replacing the 1980 constitution that was adopted during the Pinochet dictatorship. Among other changes, the new constitution would recognize a wide variety of citizen rights, replace the binomial electoral system with proportional representation, and decentralize power by providing resources and autonomy to directly elected regional governments.[26]

### *Outlook for Governance*

Bachelet and the new Chilean Congress, controlled by her Nueva Mayoría coalition, are scheduled to take office on March 11, 2014. She has pledged to quickly move forward with her policy agenda. Simple majorities in the legislature should allow Bachelet to enact fiscal reform and a number of other policy changes from her campaign platform, such as stronger consumer protections, union-empowering labor reforms, and the creation of a state-run pension fund to compete with private retirement plans.[27]

Other changes, including education reform and constitutional reform, require congressional supermajorities, and thus Bachelet will need to reach out to unaffiliated and Alianza legislators in order to fulfill her campaign promises. Education reform requires four-sevenths majorities in both houses of the Chilean Congress. If Bachelet is able to hold together her ideologically diverse coalition, she would need to win the support of two additional deputies and one additional senator. While many analysts think Bachelet should be able to push through her education initiative, constitutional reform is likely to be more difficult. Changes to the electoral system require three-fifths majorities in both houses, and other constitutional reforms require the support of two-thirds of the members of the Chilean Congress.[28]

There are some indications that Alianza legislators may be willing to work with Bachelet on electoral and constitutional reform. Over the past year, members of the more moderate party within the Alianza, the RN, have expressed support for ending the binomial electoral system. Likewise, several RN legislators have demonstrated an interest in moving toward the political center since the election; three deputies have formed a new party within the coalition and one senator has left the Alianza.[29] It is unclear, however, whether this sentiment is shared by a sufficient number of legislators or if Bachelet will be able to negotiate reforms that are acceptable to politicians ranging from the far left of her coalition to the center-right of the opposition. If Bachelet is unable to demonstrate that she is making progress in addressing citizen demands and implementing her agenda, most of which has broad public support,[30] Chileans may return to the streets.

## Economic Situation

According to many analysts, Chile has the most competitive and fundamentally sound economy in Latin America.[31] In 2012, Chile had a GDP of $268.2 billion and a per capita GDP of $15,410—the highest in the region.[32] Chile's current success is partially the result of the market-oriented economic policies the country has pursued over the past several decades, which have attracted foreign investment and fostered export-led development. Chile has implemented trade agreements with some 60 countries,[33] and now has open and reciprocal access to major consumer markets such as China, the European Union, and the United States. In 2012, Chile attracted $30.3 billion in foreign direct investment,[34] and enjoyed a trade surplus of $6.2 billion.[35]

The Chilean economy has also benefitted from institutionalized countercyclical fiscal policies that have helped mitigate the effects of external shocks. Under the country's fiscal responsibility law, an independent expert panel estimates cyclically adjusted government revenues based on factors such as potential GDP growth and the medium-term price of copper. The government then sets its budget to achieve a fiscal surplus of 0.5% of GDP over the medium term. When revenues exceed the fiscal target, savings are invested in sovereign wealth funds that can be drawn upon during economic downturns.[36]

## Crises and Recovery

As a result of its solid policy framework and several years of high copper prices, Chile had significant savings on hand when its economy began to slow as a result of the global financial crisis in late 2008. In early 2009, the government used funds from one of its sovereign wealth funds, the "Economic and Social Stabilization Fund," to finance a $4 billion (2.3% of GDP) economic stimulus package. The stimulus, which included temporary tax cuts for small businesses, larger transfer payments for poor Chileans, $700 million for infrastructure projects, and $1 billion for the state-owned copper company, Codelco (*Corporación Nacional del Cobre*),[37] helped Chile return to quarter-on-quarter economic growth by the end of 2009 and limit the annual economic contraction to 0.9%.[38]

Just as the Chilean economy was beginning to recover from the global financial crisis, the country was hit by a massive earthquake of magnitude 8.8 in February 2010.[39] The earthquake and subsequent tsunami killed 551 people and caused nearly $30 billion (15% of GDP) in damages.[40] In the aftermath of the earthquake, the Chilean government was able to once again draw on the Economic and Social Stabilization Fund in order to partially finance an $8.4 billion reconstruction plan.[41] The reconstruction effort is scheduled to conclude in March 2014.

Although Chile's economy suffered in the first quarter of 2010 as a result of the earthquake, it quickly recovered. Reconstruction, combined with increased investment and private consumption, helped fuel economic growth of 5.7% in 2010, 5.8% in 2011, and 5.6% in 2012.[42] The IMF estimates that GDP growth slowed to 4.4% in 2013,[43] but unemployment has fallen to a historically low rate of 5.7% and real wages have risen 4% over the past year.[44] While Chile remains vulnerable to economic troubles abroad given its open economy and heavy reliance on copper exports, the Chilean government has considerable room to pursue countercyclical policies should global conditions deteriorate; general government gross debt remains relatively low (12.9% of GDP),[45] and the country's Economic and Social Stabilization Fund holds $15.6 billion (5.8% of GDP).[46]

## Social Conditions

Strong economic growth and targeted social programs have produced considerable improvements in development indicators in Chile over the past two decades. The percentage of Chileans living in poverty fell from 38.8% in 1989 to 14.4% in 2011.[47] Primary education is now almost universal and secondary and tertiary attainment rates have increased rapidly.[48] Between 2007 and 2011, the percentage of Chileans aged 25-34 that had completed a tertiary degree increased from 32.5% to 41.3%.[49] Health indicators have also improved. The child malnutrition rate (as measured by the percentage of children under five who are underweight) is now 1%, and life expectancy is 79 years.[50] Despite these advances, several challenges remain. High levels of inequality have persisted over the past 20 years. The Gini coefficient,[51] which is used to measure income concentration, has barely moved since the mid-1990s, declining from 0.54 to 0.53. Although the Gini coefficient falls to 0.50 when taxes and government transfers are taken into account, it is well above the Organisation for Economic Cooperation and Development (OECD) average of 0.31.[52] Moreover, inter-generational social mobility is low by OECD standards, as the education system tends to replicate existing class disparities.[53] The OECD maintains that "as the economy advances further, the well-being of Chileans would benefit from expanding access to high-quality education, health care, and efficient social protection programmes."[54] As noted above, President Piñera has implemented several incremental policy reforms designed to increase social mobility, and President-elect Bachelet has proposed a series of more far-reaching initiatives designed to reduce inequality and improve public services (see "Political Situation").

# U.S.-Chile Relations

The United States and Chile have enjoyed friendly relations since Chile reestablished democratic governance in 1990. Over the past five years, the

Obama Administration has sought to maintain close ties with Chile while encouraging its leadership in Latin America. Administration officials have engaged in frequent high level meetings with their Chilean counterparts. In June 2013, President Obama hosted President Piñera at the White House. During the meeting, President Obama asserted that "the relationship between the United States and Chile is as strong and as important as any of the relationships that we have."[55] Piñera's visit also coincided with the State Department's announcement that it was nominating Chile for the Visa Waiver Program. Once Chile formally enters the program, Chilean citizens will be allowed to travel to the United States for up to 90 days without a visa.[56] Other areas of U.S.-Chilean cooperation include bilateral and regional initiatives to strengthen trade and investment ties, efforts to foster security and stability in the hemisphere, and the development of clean energy resources.

## U.S. Assistance

Although Chile was once a major recipient of U.S. foreign aid, it currently receives only minor security assistance as a result of its relatively advanced level of development. In an attempt to promote economic development and prevent the election of a communist government, the United States provided Chile with extensive assistance during the 1950s and 1960s. President Kennedy made Chile the centerpiece of his "Alliance for Progress," providing the country with over $1.7 billion (constant 2011 dollars) in overt economic assistance between 1961 and 1963.[57] Assistance declined following the 1970 election of Socialist President Salvador Allende and has generally remained low since then, increasing briefly during the early years of the Pinochet dictatorship and again following the transition to democracy. Chile received about $1.3 million in U.S. assistance in FY2011, $1.2 million in FY2012, and an estimated $1 million in FY2013.

U.S. assistance for Chile in FY2014 is currently unclear since Congress has yet to adopt a full year appropriations bill.[58] The Obama Administration has requested $1.1 million for Chile this fiscal year. The majority of the assistance ($810,000) would focus on modernizing the Chilean military, increasing its interoperability with U.S. forces, and building its capacity to participate in regional security and peacekeeping operations. The rest of the aid ($290,000) would be used to support Chilean efforts to develop and implement a comprehensive export control system.[59]

## Commercial Ties

The United States and Chile signed a bilateral trade agreement in June 2003, and President Bush signed the U.S.-Chile Free Trade Implementation Act (P.L. 108-77) into law in September of the same year.[60] Under the agreement, the United States and Chile immediately eliminated tariffs on 87% of bilateral trade. All trade in consumer and industrial goods was duty free as of 2013, and most remaining agricultural tariffs will be eliminated by 2015.[61] In the absence of the trade agreement, each nation's exports would be subject to the other's most-favored nation tariff rates. In 2012, Chile's average applied most-favored nation tariff was 6%, while that of the United States was 3.4%.[62] The agreement thus provides each country with preferential access to the other's market.

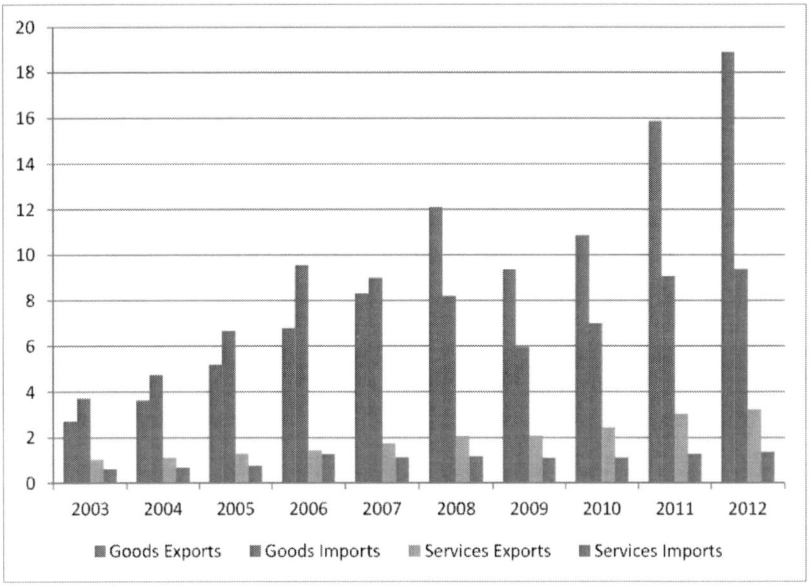


Source: CRS presentation of U.S. Department of Commerce data.

Figure 3. U.S. Trade with Chile: 2003-2012. (In billions of U.S. dollars).

Total bilateral trade more than tripled to $32.9 billion between 2004, when the U.S.-Chile Free Trade Agreement entered into force, and 2012 (see **Figure 3**). The United States now enjoys a large trade surplus in both goods and services with Chile. U.S. goods exports to Chile were valued at $18.9 billion in 2012, with refined oil products, heavy machinery, and motor vehicles accounting for a majority. U.S. goods imports from Chile have not increased as quickly as exports, as they fell between 2007 and 2009 during the global financial crisis and U.S. recession and have yet to fully recover. In 2012, U.S. goods imports from Chile were valued at $9.4 billion, with top products including copper, edible fruit, and seafood.[63] In 2012, U.S. services exports to Chile totaled $3.2 billion and U.S. services imports from Chile totaled $1.4 billion. Travel and transportation and business, professional, and technical services were the top categories for both exports and imports in U.S.-Chile services trade.[64]

In addition to the bilateral trade agreement, Chile and the United States are both participating in negotiations concerning the potential Trans-Pacific Partnership (TPP) agreement. The TPP is a proposed Asia-Pacific regional trade agreement that would include Australia, Brunei, Canada, Japan, Malaysia, Mexico, New Zealand, Peru, Singapore, and Vietnam as well as Chile and the United States.[65] Although the Piñera Administration has spoken in favor of the TPP, many Chilean analysts and policy makers—including President-elect Bachelet—have expressed concerns about the potential agreement.[66] They argue that since Chile already has trade agreements with each of the other participating nations, it should only sign onto the TPP if it provides more favorable conditions. Some worry that the agreement could serve as an indirect renegotiation of Chile's existing trade agreement with the United States, and that it could lead to concessions on issues like copyrights and pharmaceutical patents that would restrict the country's autonomy to determine public policies that benefit Chilean producers, exporters, and consumers.

### *Intellectual Property Rights Protection*

The U.S. Trade Representative (USTR), U.S. business groups, and some Members of Congress have expressed concerns about Chile's protection of intellectual property rights. Chile has been on USTR's Priority Watch List since 2007 as a result of what USTR considers the country's insufficient protection efforts. Chile reportedly took some legislative steps to improve intellectual property rights protection in 2012, but USTR "continues to have serious concerns regarding outstanding IPR issues" under the U.S.-Chile Free Trade Agreement.[67] U.S. business groups, for example, have called for increased protection for pharmaceutical patent holders and strengthened procedures for removing Internet content that infringes on copyrights.[68] Likewise, some Members of Congress have called on USTR to initiate formal dispute settlement proceedings against Chile.[69] The Chilean government maintains that it complies with all of its intellectual property rights obligations but has stated that it is open to perfecting its legal framework.[70] USTR intends to continue working with Chile, including through TPP negotiations, to resolve outstanding issues.[71] As noted above, some Chilean analysts and policy makers maintain Chile should walk away from the TPP agreement if it imposes stricter IPR standards than those Chile has already negotiated in previous trade agreements.

***Foreign Direct Investment and Bilateral Income Tax Treaty***

Foreign direct investment between Chile and the United States currently flows mostly in one direction, towards Chile. As of 2012, the accumulated stock of U.S. foreign direct investment in Chile was $39.9 billion. In comparison, the accumulated stock of Chilean foreign direct investment in the United States was $414 million.[72]

On February 4, 2010, the United States and Chile signed an income tax treaty designed to encourage investment in both countries by providing certainty on the tax treatment of investors and reducing tax-related barriers to investment. Among other provisions, the treaty would reduce source-country withholding taxes on certain cross-border payments of dividends, interest, and royalties; establish rules to determine when an enterprise or individual of one country is subject to tax on business activities in the other; enhance the mobility of labor by coordinating the tax aspects of the U.S. and Chilean pension systems; foster collaboration to resolve tax disputes and relieve double taxation; and ensure the full exchange between the U.S. and Chilean tax authorities of information for tax purposes.

The agreement, known as the "Convention Between the Government of the United States of America and the Government of the Republic of Chile for the Avoidance of Double Taxation and the Prevention of Fiscal Evasion with Respect to Taxes on Income and Capital," was submitted to the U.S. Senate for its advice and consent on May 17, 2012 (Treaty Doc. 112-8).[73] If ratified, it would be the first bilateral income tax treaty between the United States and Chile and only the second U.S. tax treaty with a South American country.[74] According to press reports, the treaty has yet to move forward because a Senator concerned about the privacy of U.S. citizens' tax data has placed a hold on all pending tax treaties.[75]

## Regional Stability

Since its return to democracy, Chile's foreign policy has been based on respect for international law, equality among states, peaceful dispute resolution, and non-interference in the internal affairs of other countries.[76] Although the country's initiatives in the international arena have often focused on forging trade and investment linkages, Chile also has been an active participant in multilateral efforts to advance peace and stability in the Western Hemisphere. For example, the Chilean government has engaged in diplomatic efforts to resolve a number of political crises in the region in recent years, and is currently one of four countries assisting with peace talks between the Colombian government and the Revolutionary Armed Forces of Colombia (*Fuerzas Armadas Revolucionarias de Colombia*, FARC)—a leftist guerilla group.[77] In October 2013, Chile was elected to a two-year term on the U.N. Security Council.

Chile has also promoted regional cooperation on peacekeeping and humanitarian relief efforts. The country quickly responded to the U.N. Security Council's March 2004 request for peacekeepers in Haiti following the collapse of Jean-Bertrand Aristide's government. This early commitment encouraged a number of other Latin American countries to contribute troops to the U.N. Stabilization Mission in Haiti (MINUSTAH), establishing an opportunity for regional political and military cooperation and integration. Chile has committed more human and material resources to MINUSTAH than it has to any previous peacekeeping mission,[78] and still has 462 soldiers and 14 police on the ground as Haiti continues to recover from the massive earthquake that struck the country in January 2010.[79] In October 2012, Chile sponsored a disaster response initiative at the 10th Conference of the Defense Ministers of the Americas. The initiative, which was backed by the United States and adopted at the conference, creates a coordination mechanism to improve the region's collective response to humanitarian emergencies.[80]

Additionally, Chile is working with the United States on citizen security and antidrug efforts in Central America—a region struggling with high levels of crime and violence.[81] Both countries are part of the Group of Friends of Central America, which has worked with Central American governments to design and implement a regional security strategy. Among other initiatives, Chile is supporting police reform in Honduras and providing military training in Guatemala.[82] Chile is also participating in Operation *Martillo*, a multinational and interagency drug interdiction effort designed to cut off illicit trafficking routes along the Atlantic and Pacific coasts of Central America.[83]

## Clean Energy Development

The U.S. and Chilean governments have both expressed interest in developing clean energy resources to meet domestic needs and mitigate global climate change. Chile has become more reliant on carbon-emitting power sources (such as coal-fired thermoelectric plants) in recent years, however, as the country has struggled to satisfy its fast-growing demand for energy, which is expected to double over the next decade and triple by 2032.[84] Although Chile adopted a law in 2013 that requires 20% of the country's electricity to be generated from nonconventional renewable energy sources by 2025, only about 5% of Chile's power generation currently comes from such sources.[85] President-elect Bachelet has set a goal of generating 30% of Chile's electricity from nonconventional renewable energy sources by 2030.[86]

The United States is currently working with Chile to overcome the financial and technical barriers that have prevented the country from taking advantage of its vast wind, solar, tidal, and geothermal energy potential. In June 2009, under the umbrella of President Obama's "Energy and Climate Partnership for the Americas," the United States and Chile signed a memorandum of understanding on cooperation in clean energy technologies. As a result of the agreement, the U.S. Department of Energy has provided support to Chile's Renewable Energy Center and two solar plant pilot projects in the Atacama Desert. Future bilateral collaboration is likely to involve biofuels, biomass, wind, and geothermal energy projects.[87] In addition to supporting energy development in Chile, these technical cooperation initiatives provide those involved with information and best practices that can be applied in the United States.

# Appendix. Chilean Political Party Acronyms

**Table A-1. Chilean Political Acronyms**

| Acronym | Political Party | Description |
|---|---|---|
| PC | Communist Party | Left-wing member party of Nueva Mayoría.[a] |
| PDC | Christian Democratic Party | Centrist member party of Nueva Mayoría. |
| PL | Liberal Party | Centrist party created by PPD dissidents. |

| Acronym | Political Party | Description |
|---|---|---|
| | | It was formerly known as Chile Primero, or "Chile First." |
| PPD | Party for Democracy | Center-left member party of Nueva Mayoría. |
| PRI | Regionalist Party of Independents | Centrist party formed in a merger of regional parties. |
| PRSD | Social Democratic Radical Party | Center-left member party of Nueva Mayoría. |
| PS | Socialist Party | Center-left member party of Nueva Mayoría. |
| RN | National Renewal | Center-right member party of the Alianza.[b] |
| UDI | Independent Democratic Union | Right-wing member party of the Alianza. |

Source: CRS.

Notes:

[a] *Nueva Mayoría*, or "New Majority," is a center-left coalition of parties. It replaced the political coalition known as the *Concertación*.

[b] The *Alianza,* or "Alliance for Chile," is a center-right coalition of parties.

## End Notes

[1] World Bank, "Chile: Data," http://data.worldbank.org/country/chile.

[2] *Chile: A Country Study*, ed. Rex A. Hudson (Washington, DC: Library of Congress, 1994).

[3] *Informe de la Comisión Nacional de Verdad y Reconciliación*, February 1991; *Informe Sobre Calificación de Víctimas de Violaciones de Derechos Humanos y la Violencia Política*, September 1996; *Informe de la Comisión Nacional Sobre Prisión Política y Tortura*, November 2004; *Informe de la Comisión Asesora para la Calificación de Detenidos Desaparecidos, Ejecutados Políticos y Víctimas de Prisión Política y Tortura*, August 2011.

[4] Alan Angell and Benny Pollack, "The Chilean Elections of 1989 and the Politics of the Transition to Democracy," *Bulletin of Latin American Research*, Volume 9 (1), 1990.

[5] Patricio Navia and Ricardo Godoy, "From Pinochet to Piñera: The Alianza's Quest to Democratically Win Power in Chile," paper delivered at the 2012 Latin American Studies Association Conference in San Francisco, CA, May 23-26, 2012.

[6] Oscar Landerretch, "Chile and the Ideology of Stability," paper delivered at the 2012 Latin American Studies Association Conference, San Francisco, CA, May 23-26, 2012.

[7] "El País que Entrega la Concertación Dos Décadas Después de Asumir el Mando," *El Mercurio*, January 18, 2010; Gobierno de Chile, Ministerio de Planificación, "CASEN 2009: Situación de Pobreza a Nivel de Personas, Según Región," 2010.

[8] Biblioteca del Congreso Nacional de Chile, *Las Reformas a la Constitución de 1980*, August 9, 2005.

[9] Marny A. Requa, "A Human Rights Triumph? Dictatorship-era Crimes and the Chilean Supreme Court," *Human Rights Law Review*, vol. 12, no. 1 (2012), pp. 79-106.

[10] Amnesty International, "Chile: 40 Years on from Pinochet's Coup, Impunity Must End," September 10, 2013.

[11] Although the center-right coalition ran under the banner of the "Coalition for Change" in 2009, Chileans generally continue to refer to it by its historic name, the "Alliance for Chile" or *Alianza*.

[12] Piñera was the leading vote-getter in the first round, winning the support of 44% of the electorate. He was followed by Frei at 30% and two Concertación dissidents, Marco Enríquz-Ominami and Jorge Arrate, at 20% and 6%, respectively. "Chile: Piñera Wins the Second Round," *Latin American Regional Report: Brazil & Southern Cone*, February 2010.

[13] President Sebastián Piñera, "Chile Cumple y Avanza Hacia el Desarollo," Tercera Cuenta Pública a la Nación, May 21, 2012.

[14] See, for example, Thalif Deen, "Chile: Disillusion with Pinochet-Era Political System Grows," *Inter Press Service*, January 31, 2012; Marta Lagos, *Chile Al Desnudo*, Latinobarómetro, October 28, 2011; and Sergio Bitar, "¿Que Pasa en Chile?: (2) Chile y Sus Movilizaciones: ¿Por Qué?," *Infolatam*, September 14, 2011.

[15] Patricio Navia, "Democracy to the Extent Possible in Chile," *Latin American Research Review*, Special Issue (2010).

[16] Ernesto Muñoz-Lamartine, "Student Leaders Reinvent the Protest," *Berkeley Review of Latin American Studies*, Fall 2011-Winter 2012, p. 27.

[17] Carl Meacham and Robert Funk, *Chile's 2013 Presidential Elections: Explanations and Predictions*, Center for Strategic & International Studies (CSIS), Washington, DC, December 2013, p. 4.

[18] Since a coalition must win by a two-to-one margin in order to secure both seats in an electoral district, a major swing in voters from one coalition to the other—from 60%-40% to 40%-60%, for example—will produce the exact same result. Consequently, the two major coalitions have historically split seats in more than 95% of electoral districts. Navia, 2010, op.cit.

[19] See, for example, "The Dam Breaks: Pent-Up Frustration at the Flaws of a Successful Democracy," *The Economist*, August 27, 2011; and Kailie Middleton, "Summary: 2013 Presidential Elections and Economic Outlook – What's Next for Chile?," *Americas Society/Council of the Americas*, May 9, 2013.

[20] Prior to the electoral reform, registration was voluntary but voting was mandatory for registered voters. Now, registration is automatic and voting is voluntary.

[21] "Evaluación de Gobierno Diciembre 2013," *Adimark GfK*, January 7, 2014.

[22] Servicio Electoral de Chile, *Ultimo Boletín Informativo de Resultados Preliminares*, December 15, 2013.

[23] Servicio Electoral de Chile, *Boletín de Resultados Provisorios, Elección Presidente de la República 2013, Colegios Escrutadores*, November 21, 2013.

[24] "Nueva Mayoría Wins a Majority in Congress," *Economist Intelligence Unit*, November 29, 2013.

[25] "Bachelet and Concertación Fall Just Short in Chile," *Latin American Weekly Report*, November 21, 2013; "Vuelco en el Distrito 56: Nueva Mayoría Pierde Doblaje Tras Último Cómputo," *El Mercurio*, November 22, 2013; "In Brief – Chile: Horvath Launches New Movement," *Latin News Daily Report*, December 20, 2013.

[26] *Chile de Todos*, Programa de Gobierno de Michelle Bachelet: 2014-2018, October 2013.

[27] For more information on Chile's pension system, see CRS Report R42449, *Chile's Pension System: Background in Brief.*

[28] Kristen Sehnbruch and Peter M. Siavelis, "Why Victory for Bachelet in Chile is Undeniable but Bittersweet," *Washington Post,* November 26, 2013.

[29] "Chile's RN Implodes," *Latin News Daily Report*, January 8, 2014.

[30] Centro de Estudios Públicos (CEP), *Estudio Nacional de Opinión Pública Nº 70*, October 2013.

[31] See, for example, *Global Competitiveness Report 2013-2014*, ed. Klaus Schwab (Geneva: World Economic Forum, 2013); and "Chile: Country Report," *Economist Intelligence Unit*, November 2013.

[32] International Monetary Fund (IMF), *2013 Article IV Consultation*, Country Report No.13/198, July 2013, p.29.

[33] Gobierno de Chile, Ministerio de Relaciones Exteriores, "Tratados de Libre Comercio: Acuerdos Comerciales Vigentes," http://www.direcon.gob.cl/acuerdo/list.

[34] U.N. Economic Commission for Latin America and the Caribbean, *Foreign Direct Investment in Latin America and the Caribbean, 2012*, May 2013, http://www.eclac.cl/publicaciones /xml/4/49844/ ForeignDirectInvestmentBriefPaper2012.pdf.

[35] Chile Customs data, as made available by *Global Trade Atlas*, May 2013.

[36] "Chile's Upcoming Political Cycle: Tackling Social Challenges and the Income Inequality Gap," *IHS Global Insight*, December 9, 2013.

[37] "Chile's Economy: Stimulating," *The Economist*, February 19, 2009.

[38] "Chile Economy: Quick View—Out of Recession," *Economist Intelligence Unit*, November 20, 2009; IMF, July 2013, op. cit.

[39] For more information on the Chile earthquake, see CRS Report R41112, *Chile Earthquake: U.S. and International Response*, by June S. Beittel and Rhoda Margesson.

[40] President Sebastián Piñera, "Chile Cumple y Avanza Hacia el Desarollo," Tercera Cuenta Pública a la Nación, May 21, 2012; "Chile: Country Report," *Economist Intelligence Unit*, September 2010.

[41] Simon Gardner, "Post-Quake Rebuild Fuels Chile Recovery a Year On," *Reuters*, February 25, 2011.

[42] IMF, July 2013, op.cit., p.29.

[43] IMF, *World Economic Outlook: Transitions and Tensions*, October 2013, p.69.

[44] Banco Central de Chile, *Avance Estadístico del Boletín Mensual*, January 7, 2014.

[45] IMF, "World Economic Outlook Database, October 2013," November 2013.

[46] Government of Chile, Ministry of Finance, *Monthly Report of the Economic and Social Stabilization Fund*, November 2013.

[47] "El País que Entrega la Concertación Dos Décadas Después de Asumir el Mando," *El Mercurio*, January 18, 2010; Randall Woods, "Chilean Poverty Rate Resumes Downward Path as Economy Expands, *Businessweek*, July 20, 2012.

[48] Nicola Brandt, *Chile: Climbing on Giants' Shoulders: Better Schools for All Chilean Children*, Organization for Economic Cooperation and Development (OECD), OECD Economics Department Working Papers No. 784, 2010.

[49] OECD, *OECD.Stat*, 2012.

[50] World Bank, "Chile: Data," http://data.worldbank.org/country/chile.

[51] The Gini coefficient is the most commonly used measure of inequality. A value of 0.0 represents absolute equality and a value of 1.0 represents absolute inequality.

[52] OECD, "Income Distribution," *OECD Social and Welfare Statistics*, 2013.

[53] OECD, *OECD Economic Surveys: Chile*, January 2012; "UNESCO: Sistema Educativo Chileno Fomenta la Disigualdad," *La Nación* (Chile), December 5, 2011.

[54] OECD, *OECD Economic Surveys: Chile*, October 2013.

[55] "President Barack Obama Holds a Media Availability with Chilean President Sebastian Piñera – Media Availability," *CQ Transcriptions*, June 4, 2013.

[56] For more information on the Visa Waiver Program, see CRS Report RL32221, *Visa Waiver Program*, by Alison Siskin.

[57] U.S. Agency for International Development (USAID), *U.S. Overseas Loans and Grants: Obligations and Loan Authorizations, July 1, 1945-September 30, 2011*, http://gbk.eads.usaidallnet.gov/index.html.

[58] Congress passed the Continuing Appropriations Act, 2014 (H.R. 2775) on October 16, 2013, and President Obama signed it into law (P.L. 113-46) on October 17, 2013. The continuing resolution continues FY2013 foreign operations funding levels, including previous sequestration and rescission reductions, until January 15, 2014. For more information, see CRS Report R43043, *State, Foreign Operations, and Related Programs: FY2014 Budget and Appropriations*, by Susan B. Epstein, Alex Tiersky, and Marian L. Lawson.

[59] U.S. Department of State, *Congressional Budget Justification for Foreign Operations, Fiscal Year 2012*, April 8, 2011; *Congressional Budget Justification for Foreign Operations, Fiscal Year 2013*, March 9, 2012; *Congressional Budget Justification for Foreign Operations, Fiscal Year 2014*, May 17, 2013; and "Department of State and U.S. Agency for International Development FY2013 Post-Sequester 653(a) Initial Allocations," 2013.

[60] For more information on the U.S.-Chile Free Trade Agreement, see CRS Report RL31144, *The U.S.-Chile Free Trade Agreement: Economic and Trade Policy Issues*, by J. F. Hornbeck.

[61] U.S. Trade Representative (USTR), *2012 National Trade Estimate Report on Foreign Trade Barriers*, March 2012.

[62] World Trade Organization (WTO), "Trade and Tariff Indicators," http://www.wto.org/english /res_e/statis_e/ statis_maps_e.htm.

[63] U.S. Department of Commerce data, as made available by the U.S. International Trade Commission, November 2013.

[64] U.S. Department of Commerce data, as made available by the Bureau of Economic Analysis, November 2013.

[65] For more information on the Trans-Pacific Partnership agreement, see CRS Report R42694, *The Trans-Pacific Partnership (TPP) Negotiations and Issues for Congress*, coordinated by Ian F. Fergusson and CRS Report R42344, *Trans-Pacific Partnership (TPP) Countries: Comparative Trade and Economic Analysis*, by Brock R. Williams.

[66] See: *Chile de Todos*, Programa de Gobierno de Michelle Bachelet: 2014-2018, October 2013, p. 154; Francisca Skoknic, "Wikileaks: Nueva Filtración Devela los Alcances de la Negociación del Tratado Secreto TPP," *Centro de Investigación Periodística (CIPER)*, November 13, 2013; Sergio Bitar and Jorge Heine, "Chile y el Acuerdo TransPacífico," *El Mercurio*, November 26, 2013; and A. Chávez and P. Ojeda, "Los Desafíos de la Administración Bachelet en Materia de Relaciones Internacionales," *Diario Financiero* (Chile), December 26, 2013.

[67] USTR, *2013 Special 301 Report*, May 2013, http://www.ustr.gov/sites/default/files/ 05012013%202013%20Special%20301%20Report.pdf.

[68] "IPR Groups Blast Chile for FTA Violations; Hatch Calls for Dispute Settlement," *Inside U.S. Trade*, February 24, 2012.

[69] See, for example, Letter from Orrin G. Hatch, Ranking Member of the Senate Committee on Finance, to Ambassador Ron Kirk, United States Trade Representative, February 16, 2012.

[70] "Patentes: Chile Responde Ante Acusación de Senador de EEUU," *La Nación* (Chile), February 28, 2012.

[71] USTR, May 2013, op.cit.

[72] U.S. Bureau of Economic Analysis, "Balance of Payments and Direct Investment Position Data," November 2013.

[73] The full text of the treaty, as presented to the Senate for ratification, is available at http://www.gpo.gov/fdsys/pkg/ CDOC-112tdoc8/pdf/CDOC-112tdoc8.pdf.

[74] U.S. Department of the Treasury, "U.S., Chile Sign Income Tax Treaty," Press Release, February 4, 2010.

[75] Patrick Temple-West, "U.S. Treasury Official Urges Senate Action on Tax Treaties," *Reuters*, December 12, 2013.

[76] "Reforma de la Cancillería," *El Mercurio*, June 1, 2012.

[77] For more information on the Colombian peace negotiations, see CRS Report R42982, *Peace Talks in Colombia*, by June S. Beittel.

[78] Enzo Di Nocera García and Ricardo Benavente Cresta, "Chile: Responding to a Regional Crisis," in *Capacity Building for Peacekeeping: The Case of Haiti*, eds. John T. Fishel and Andrés Sáenz, pp.66-90 (Dulles, VA: Potomac Books, 2007).

[79] United Nations, "U.N. Mission's Summary Detailed by Country," November 30, 2013.

[80] Cheryl Pellerin, "Panetta Reaffirms Partnership, Friendship with Chile," *Armed Forces Press Service*, April 26, 2012; Leon Panetta, "Hemisphere Improves Disaster Response Operation," *Miami Herald*, November 6, 2012.

[81] For more information on security issues in Central America, see CRS Report R41731, *Central America Regional Security Initiative: Background and Policy Issues for Congress*, by Peter J. Meyer and Clare Ribando Seelke.

[82] Noé Leiva, "EEUU, Chile y Colombia Asesoran a Honduras en Lucha Contra el Crimen," *Agence France Presse*, January 19, 2012; "Ejército de Chile Entrenará a Soldados Guatemaltecos para Mejorar Seguridad," *Agence France Presse*, September 17, 2013.

[83] Cheryl Pellerin, April 2012, op.cit.

[84] "Chile Industry: Energy Security Still Elusive," *Economist Intelligence Unit*, April 21, 2011.

[85] Juliette Kerr, "Chilean Congress Approves New Renewables Law," *IHS Global Insight*, September 5, 2013.

[86] *Chile de Todos*, Programa de Gobierno de Michelle Bachelet: 2014-2018, October 2013, p. 48.

[87] White House, Office of the Press Secretary, "The United States and Chile: Environment, Energy, and Climate Change," Fact Sheet, March 21, 2011.

In: Chile
Editor: Garrett M. Ulrich

ISBN: 978-1-61122-031-5


*Chapter 2*

# CHILE'S PENSION SYSTEM: BACKGROUND IN BRIEF*

*Alison M. Shelton*

## SUMMARY

In 1980, Chile was the first country to replace its pay-as-you-go public pension system with a system of individual accounts. The "Chilean model" has been widely studied as one possible model for public pension restructuring.

Chile's public pension system consists of three tiers: a poverty prevention tier, an individual account tier, and a voluntary savings tier. The poverty prevention tier provides a minimum benefit to aged persons who did not participate in the public pension system and to retired workers whose monthly pensions financed by individual account assets (the second tier) do not reach certain thresholds. Workers contribute 10% of wage or salary income to an individual account in the second tier and choose a private-sector Administradora de Fondos de Pensiones (AFP) with which to invest their pension contributions. Employers are not required to contribute to employees' AFPs, although since 2008 employers have been required to pay the premiums for workers' survivor and disability insurance, which are provided by private insurance companies. Upon retirement, the worker may withdraw assets that have accumulated in the individual account as an immediate or deferred

* This is an edited, reformatted and augmented version of Congressional Research Service Publication, No. R42449, dated March 28, 2012.

annuity or through programmed withdrawals. The third tier allows workers to supplement retirement income with voluntary, tax-favored savings.

In 2008, Chile approved major reforms intended, among other goals, to increase participation in the public pension system, improve competition among the private-sector individual account managers, and bolster the poverty prevention tier. There has been concern that, as a result of low participation rates and underreporting, many workers could reach retirement with individual account balances that are too small to provide an adequate pension annuity. The 2008 reforms helped address these concerns by expanding the poverty prevention tier, phasing in coverage for most self-employed workers, and providing incentives for additional voluntary saving through the system's third tier. Other provisions approved in 2008 are intended to reduce high investment management fees (administrative costs) by increasing competition among AFPs.

## INTRODUCTION

In 1980, Chile replaced its pay-as-you-go public pension system, under which benefits for current beneficiaries were paid with taxes from current workers, similar to Social Security in the United States, with a system of individual accounts that has become a possible model for public pension restructuring around the world. The preceding pay-as-you-go system had been foundering financially and was unable to pay full scheduled benefits. In addition, the previous system had been extremely complex, with more than 100 different combinations of contribution rates, retirement ages, and benefit amounts for different groups of employees.

Chile's system of private pension accounts has been widely studied as one model for public pension restructuring. The U.S. Congress has considered a number of proposals to include private accounts in the Social Security system, either by carving contributions to private accounts out of Social Security's current payroll tax revenue stream or by adding private accounts onto Social Security's traditional benefit system.

This report provides an overview of Chile's pension system, including a description of major reforms approved in 2008, the Chilean government's role, and challenges facing the system. The Chilean pension system consists of three tiers: a poverty prevention tier, an individual account tier, and a voluntary savings tier. The poverty prevention tier provides a basic benefit to aged persons who did not participate in the public pension system and to retired workers whose monthly pensions financed by individual account assets (the second tier) do not reach certain thresholds. Under the second tier, workers contribute 10% of wage or salary income to an individual account and choose a private-sector Administradora de Fondos de Pensiones (AFP) to manage the account. Upon retirement, the worker may withdraw the individual account's accumulated assets as an immediate or deferred annuity or through programmed withdrawals. A third, voluntary savings tier encourages workers to supplement pension income with additional savings. The 2008 reforms were designed, among other goals, to increase participation in the public pension system, reduce high investment management fees and administrative costs, and bolster the poverty prevention tier.[1]

# PENSION STRUCTURE: THREE TIERS

## First Tier: Poverty Prevention

The first tier of Chile's public pension system is a poverty prevention tier funded by general revenues. The poverty prevention tier is available to all citizens aged 65 and older who pass a means test and who have lived in Chile for at least 20 years, and for at least 3 of the past 5 years, whether or not they contributed to an individual account (the second tier).[2]

The Chilean government pays a Basic Solidarity Pension to individuals who have not contributed to individual accounts and pass the means test. The Basic Solidarity Pension is 75,000 Chilean pesos (about $154) per month, wage indexed starting from July 2008.[3]

A Pension Solidarity Complement is paid to individuals who contributed to individual accounts (the second tier) and pass the means test, but who would receive a monthly pension below a threshold amount of 255,000 Chilean pesos (about $523) in July 2011, wage indexed thereafter. In the case of retirees who have annuitized their individual account balances, the Pension Solidarity Complement is paid as the difference between the minimum benefit amount and the annuity financed by the individual account. In the case of pensions paid through programmed withdrawals from the individual account, the Pension Solidarity Component is paid once the member has used the balance in his or her individual account. Because the existence of a poverty prevention tier could discourage savings through the second tier (individual accounts), the state's contributions are designed so that every dollar saved always increases retirement income, but not by a full dollar.[4]

## Second Tier: Mandatory Individual Accounts

### *Pension Contribution Rates*

Employees are required to contribute 10% of wage and salary earnings to an individual account, up to a ceiling on monthly taxable earnings of 60 unidades de fomento (UF).[5] Since 2009, the earnings ceiling has been indexed to growth in average earnings and stood at 67.4 UF in early 2012.[6] Employers are required to withhold workers' contributions from their paychecks and to forward contributions to the AFP chosen by each worker. Employees' contributions are tax deferred: contributions do not count as income in the period they are made and interest earnings are exempt from taxation until withdrawal. Retirees pay regular income taxes on pension income when it is drawn as a retirement benefit.[7]

Employers are not generally required to contribute to employees' accounts. Since 2008, employers have been required to pay premiums for survivor and disability insurance, which in Chile is provided by private insurance companies. Survivor and disability insurance premiums have recently totaled about 1.49% of employers' payroll, on average.[8] Tax incentives are available to employers who make matching contributions to employees' supplemental savings through the third, voluntary savings tier.

### *Structure of Individual Accounts*

Workers choose one AFP with which to invest their 10% pension contributions. An AFP is a private company that is regulated by Chile's Superintendent of Pensions. An AFP exclusively manages a worker's pension investments and administers pension benefits, including collecting pension contributions, keeping records, managing pension investments, calculating retirement annuities (unless a worker chooses to contract with an insurance company), and paying retirement annuities.

Workers may choose any AFP and may switch AFPs at any time for a fee. In February 2012, there were six AFPs. Each AFP offers up to five government-approved funds, called Funds A to E, with different levels of risk. Fund A, with the highest proportion of equities, carries the highest risk and potentially the highest return. The five-fund portfolios operate within regulations established separately for each type of fund concerning the credit rating and liquidity of investments, diversification, and other factors.

Participants pay administrative charges to the AFPs for managing individual account assets. These charges are levied in addition to the 10% mandatory contribution. The AFPs are free to set fees and commissions, as long as these are standard for all members. In other words, it has been assumed that participants' freedom to choose their AFPs, combined with competition among AFPs, will result in an appropriate level of commissions. Administrative charges and AFP profits have historically been significant, however.[9]

***Retirement Benefits from Individual Accounts***

A worker's pension annuity is calculated based on the accumulated assets, plus returns, in his or her individual account. The annuity calculation is based on age and gender-specific life expectancy. If the pension annuity is below certain thresholds, the Chilean government provides additional payments to bring the total pension up to the monthly Solidarity Pension (first tier) amount.

Early retirement is possible at any time as long as the capital accumulated in the account is sufficient to finance a pension that (1) starting from August 2010, replaces 70% of the worker's average earnings in the 10 years prior to drawing the pension, and (2) starting from July 2012, equals 80% of the Pension Solidarity Complement. The normal retirement age (NRA) is reduced by one or two years for each five years of work in certain specified, arduous occupations, with a maximum reduction in the NRA of 10 years.

The assets accumulated in the individual account can be withdrawn in the following ways:

1) *Programmed Withdrawal.* The AFP calculates monthly annuity amounts, including an annual inflation adjustment, and manages the pension payments. The account balance is held in one of the three lower-risk funds, at the retiree's choice, to avoid risk-taking that might result in premature account exhaustion and trigger the government's minimum benefit guarantee. The account holder retains ownership of the account, and can leave any remaining balance to heirs, but assumes longevity and investment risk in the case of monthly withdrawals that exceed the minimum benefit guarantee.
2) *Life Annuity.* Members may choose a life insurance company to pay an inflation-adjusted monthly pension and a survivor pension to any beneficiaries. The account holder transfers ownership of the assets to the life insurance company, which assumes both financial and longevity risk. The decision to choose a life annuity is irrevocable once the ownership of the account assets has been transferred to the life insurance company.

3) *Temporary Income with Deferred Life Annuity.* The account holder contracts with an insurance company to provide temporary or programmed monthly payments until, at some point after retirement, the insurance company starts to pay a life annuity. In this way the account holder retains ownership of the part of the account that remains in the AFP until the life annuity begins.
4) *Immediate Annuity Plus Programmed Withdrawals.* In 2004, a new option was created, under which a portion of the account balance is used to purchase an immediate annuity and the remainder is paid out as programmed withdrawals.

From the account balance, 15 UFs are reserved to cover funeral expenses.

***Disability and Survivor Benefits from Individual Accounts***

In Chile, disability and survivor benefits are financed by a combination of the worker's individual account and private insurance. AFPs are required to purchase insurance policies to finance disability and survivorship benefits on behalf of participants and their surviving dependents through the age of 65.[10] Since 2009, employers have been required to pay the premiums to the AFPs on behalf of their employees. Survivor and disability insurance premiums have recently averaged about 1.49% of payroll contributions.[11] This insurance is used to pay the difference between an annuity financed from the accumulated assets in the worker's account and the disability or survivor pension to which the disabled worker or the worker's survivor (spouse, children, or parents) is entitled.

The monthly disability pension is 70% of the worker's base salary (defined as his or her average monthly salary for the previous 10 years) for those entitled to a total disability pension and 50% of base salary for those who are entitled to a partial disability pension.[12] Eligible survivors may include a surviving widow(er)[13] and children younger than aged 18 or aged 24 if a student. There is no age limit for disabled surviving children.

## Third Tier: Voluntary Additional Saving

Workers may make voluntary additional contributions to certain savings products authorized by the Chilean government, including voluntary savings accounts managed by the AFPs, mutual funds offered by banks, and savings products offered by insurance companies. Contributors may pay up to 50 UF per month (unindexed) to voluntary savings vehicles, over and above the mandatory 10% basic contribution to the AFP. Contributions may be made on a periodic basis or on a single occasion. Contributors may transfer funds from a voluntary savings account to the individual account (tier 2) to increase the amount of the monthly pension annuity.

Voluntary contributions receive tax preferences. At the worker's choice, contributions may be paid from pre-tax income with the assets and accumulated income subject to taxation upon withdrawal, or contributions may be made out of after-tax income and are tax-free at withdrawal. Because tax preferences provide little incentive to workers who have no income tax liability, the government subsidizes low-income workers' contributions to voluntary savings accounts.

Since 2008, the government has also offered tax incentives to promote employer-sponsored voluntary pension plans (Ahorro Previsional Voluntario Colectivo). The tax incentives are intended to encourage firms to establish voluntary savings accounts for their employees and to match a share of employees' contributions.[14]

# Financial and Regulatory Role of the Chilean Government

## Role of General Revenues

The second tier of individual accounts is generally fully funded by workers' contributions. In cases in which the Superintendent closes an AFP or an AFP becomes insolvent, the Chilean government assumes responsibility for contributions, guaranteeing pension benefits, disability pensions, and the death benefit.[15] Chile's government is also responsible for financing the first, poverty prevention tier, from general revenues, including the Basic Solidarity Pension for persons who did not contribute to individual accounts and the Pension Solidarity Complement for persons whose annuitized individual accounts provide pensions below the guaranteed minimum. The Chilean government also provides subsidies to low-income workers who contribute under the third, voluntary savings tier, and tax incentives to employees who save in the third tier as well as to employers who establish voluntary savings accounts and match employees' contributions to these accounts.

Transition costs have been financed from general revenues, particularly during the first years of Chile's move from a pay-as-you-go system to a system of individual accounts plus poverty prevention programs. Between the 1981 conversion to individual accounts and 1999, total transition costs averaged about 3.25% of gross domestic product (GDP) per year.[16] Transition costs include spending for current beneficiaries and those who remained in the pay-as-you-go system, plus "recognition bonds"[17] issued to those who transferred to the new individual account system. Although expenditures on recognition bonds are currently increasing as more former pay-as-you-go system participants reach retirement age, total transition costs have begun to decline as the number of participants under the pay-as-you-go system declines and are expected to be negligible by about 2050.

The 2008 reforms discussed below, which included substantial expansions of the government-financed poverty prevention tier, are expected to cost an additional 0.5% of GDP in the first few years, rising to about 1% of GDP after phase-in by 2025.[18] This estimate is qualified, however, by considerable uncertainty in the number of potential beneficiaries in the reformed poverty prevention tier, as well as uncertainty about future demographic and economic assumptions. It is "quite possible"[19] that the current 10% contribution rate may be insufficient to fund adequate benefits from individual accounts, particularly if life expectancy increases, in which case payouts from the poverty prevention tier would increase.

## Supervision

The Superintendent of Pensions is responsible for supervising and regulating the mandatory and voluntary individual account systems. The Superintendent approves new AFPs; sets capital requirements; oversees AFP accounting, advertising, investment, and legal practices; interprets laws; issues regulations; proposes new laws; imposes fines; and orders the dissolution of AFPs when necessary. For each of the five investment portfolios that AFPs are authorized to offer, the Chilean government sets certain per-instrument, per-issuer, and per-group-of-instrument limits to ensure that the five authorized portfolios are diversified, have appropriate balances of risk and return, and that a single AFP does not acquire a controlling interest in any single issuer of stocks or bonds.[20]

## 2008 Reforms

In 2008, Chile under President Michelle Bachelet introduced several major reforms to the pension system to address concerns, including low participation rates, high pension fund management fees, and inadequate benefits for low-wage and women workers.

### Participation Rates

Before the 2008 reforms, only about 62% of the labor force, and about 68% of those employed, participated actively in the national pension system.[21] A large share of the workforce was then, and continues to be, self-employed in Chile's formal and large informal sectors. Prior to 2008, the law allowed self-employed workers to participate on a voluntary basis and only a small percentage of the self-employed chose to contribute. Other non-participants were temporarily out of the workforce due to caregiving or unemployment. Among those who did participate, many underreported their income to lower their contributions. As a result of low participation rates and underreporting, there was concern that many workers would reach retirement with individual account balances that were too small to provide an adequate pension annuity.

The 2008 reforms phased in a requirement that most self-employed workers contribute to the pension system.[22] In addition, the 2008 reform package, to increase participation among younger workers, established government subsidies to the accounts of low-income workers between the ages of 18 and 35. The 2008 reforms also tightened rules facing employers who fail to transfer workers' contributions.

### Administrative Costs

Historically, fees and commissions charged by AFPs to manage individual accounts have been a concern attributed to high-cost marketing and increased concentration in the industry.[23] The number of AFPs was 12 in 1981, rose to 21 by 1994, and declined to 5 by 2008 due to mergers and closures. Administrative costs reduce investment returns to account holders, reducing a worker's account balance over time and resulting in a lower annuity at retirement.

The 2008 reform package included a number of measures intended to reduce administrative costs, including a simplified fee structure that facilitates workers' ability to compare administrative costs among the AFPs.[24] The 2008 package also included provisions intended to increase competition among the AFPs and reduce industry concentration. Insurance companies were allowed to create AFP subsidiaries. In addition, AFPs were allowed to contract out more services, such as record keeping and customer service, in order to lower barriers to entry for new AFPs. The 2008 reforms also created a competitive bidding process under which all new participants for two years are automatically enrolled in the AFP that offers the lowest management charges in the most recent round of bidding; it is hoped that this new bidding process, by guaranteeing a steady flow of participants for two years without having to incur marketing costs, will attract potential new AFPs.

It may be too early to tell if these reforms will increase competition. In February 2012, the number of AFPs was six. In January 2012, AFP Modelo won the competitive bidding process for new workers' accounts for the next two years with a low bid of 0.77% for administrative expenses, notably lower than current AFP administrative expenses, which range from 1.14% to 2.35% of covered (that is, taxable) earnings.[25]

## Pension Benefit Adequacy

The adequacy of pension benefits has also been a source of concern. Individual accounts systems do not generally allow for the redistribution that occurs in public defined benefit systems; instead, a worker's pension is directly related to his or her own earnings and contribution history. In addition, low or negative returns between 1995 and 1998, combined with high management fees, caused many workers to lose money during this period. In 1998, the Chilean government asked workers to consider delaying retirement until the market recovered.[26]

As part of the 2008 reforms, the Chilean government restructured the poverty prevention tier to expand protection for low-income workers and workers who have contributed inconsistently, or not at all, to the individual account tier. In addition, to encourage participation in the third tier of voluntary savings, the 2008 reforms created bonuses for low-income workers and tax incentives for contributing employees and for employers who establish voluntary savings accounts and match employees' contributions to these accounts. Also in 2008, a subsidy was approved to encourage employers to hire workers between the ages of 18 and 35, on the principle that early contributions can have a significant impact on final pension amounts.

The 2008 reforms also contained several measures intended to improve the adequacy of women's benefits from their individual accounts, given that women often earn lower wages than men and many leave the workforce temporarily or permanently for caregiving. The Chilean government deposits a bonus in a woman's private account at age 65 for every live birth or adopted child. For women who have not contributed to the pension system, the Chilean government makes a corresponding increase in the amount of the Solidarity minimum benefit. The bonus is equivalent to 10% (i.e., the contribution rate) of the monthly minimum wage at the time of the child's birth, times 18 months, plus the average net rate of return on individual account pension plans in the C Fund from the child's birth until the pension is claimed. Women's contributions are boosted somewhat above the statutory 10% rate by a 2008 provision that charges both sexes the same premium for survivor and disability insurance, but deposits the difference between the higher premium that would have been charged to men into women's individual accounts. Finally, reforms passed in 2008 allow a judge to transfer up to 50% of funds from one spouse's account to the other spouse's account in cases of divorce or annulment.

## CONCLUSION

Lessons from Chile's introduction of individual accounts may be helpful to other countries considering a similar transition, although not all of Chile's experiences are directly comparable to major Organisation for Economic Co-operation and Development (OECD) countries, such as the United States. For example, Chile's experience with high administrative costs may or may not be relevant to a second country, depending on whether the second country's public or private sector would manage account investments and the extent of financial-sector competition in the second country. Another difference between Chile and other countries may be the degree of public acceptance for the first, welfare tier of the system, which creates fiscal pressures similar to those of a pay-as-you-go system. Another political consideration is that Chile in the early 1980s, under General Pinochet, had considerable latitude to impose top-down reform of the pension system. Transition costs are another issue facing a country considering a move to a Chilean-type model. When Chile transitioned to a private account system in 1981, the earlier pay-as-you-go system was chaotic, insolvent, and unfair.[27] At the same time, Chile's nonpension budget in the early 1980s was in surplus and available for financing transition costs, and high growth rates of economic growth in Chile during the 1980s reduced the burden of transition on the economy.

The 2008 reforms to the poverty prevention tier (the Solidarity tier) are generally acknowledged as the most important component of the 2008 reform package.[28] Chile's public pension system continues to face challenges after the 2008 reforms, however. Although the 2008 reforms will bring many self-employed workers into the public pension system, much of the informal sector remains outside the pension system. It remains to be seen whether reforms to AFPs will increase competition and lower costs.

## End Notes

[1] Under Chile's social insurance system, retirees receive free health care.

[2] The means test, which applies to both the Basic Solidarity Pension and the Pension Solidarity Component, is measured at the household level and is designed to determine that a beneficiary does not belong to the top 40% of the population based on income from earnings and pensions, by age and disability status.

[3] Superintendencia de Pensiones, "Pensi6n Básica Solidaria de Vejez," at http://www.spensiones.cl/573/article5784.html.

[4] Starting mid-2011, the Pension Solidarity Complement is defined as the value of the Basic Solidarity Pension of 75,000 Chilean pesos minus 29.4% times the value of the pension from the worker's individual account, where the figure of 29.4% is derived as the ratio of the Basic Solidarity Pension to a threshold of 255,000 Chilean pesos. See OECD, *Pensions at a Glance 2011*, Paris, France, p. 2011, http://dx.doi.org/10.1787/pension_glance-2011-en, p. 209. See also Social Security Administration, *Social Security Programs Throughout the World: the Americas, 2011*, at http://www.socialsecurity.gov/policy/docs /progdesc/ssptw/2010-2011/americas/chile.html and The World Bank, Reforming *the Pension Reforms: The Recent Initiatives and Actions on Pensions in Argentina and Chile*, SP Discussion Paper No. 0831, May 2008.

[5] Unidades de fomento, or UF, are real, inflation-adjusted units that have been used for a variety of purposes in Chile since 1967, including pension contributions and guaranteed benefits under the pension system, private and public loans, housing values, construction costs, and other purposes. In 2008, 60 UF were equal to eight times the minimum wage and 291% of average earnings (OECD, *Pensions at a Glance 2011*, Paris, France, p. 2011, http://dx.doi.org/10.1787/ pension_glance-2011-en, p. 208). At end-February 2012, one UF was equal to about $22.46, at http://www.uf.cl/.

[6] Superintendencia de Pensiones, *Informaçion Para Pago de Cotizaciones Previsionales*, at http://www.spensiones.cl/ safpstats/stats/inf_estadistica/cotprev.html.

[7] Some groups of workers have their own pension systems and do not participate in the individual account system. These include employees of railroads, the public sector, military and police, and seamen and port workers.

[8] Social Security Administration, *Social Security Programs Throughout the World: The Americas, 2011—Chile* at https://www.socialsecurity.gov/policy

[9] Superintendent of Pensions, *The Chilean Pension System, Fourth Edition*, p. 47, at http://www.safp.cl/573/article3523.html. See also Mauricio Soto, *Chilean Pension Reform: The Good, the Bad, and the In Between*, Center for Retirement Research at Boston College, Number 31, Boston, MA, June 2005 and Barbara E. Kritzer, Stephen J. Kay, and Tapen Sinha, "Next Generation of Individual Account Pension Reforms in Latin America," *Social Security Bulletin*, vol. 71, no. 1 (2011).

[10] Men and women pay the same fee for disability and survivorship insurance. But because men have higher risk rates than women, the cost of insurance differs by gender, and this difference is deposited in women's individual accounts. As a result, women's contributions to their pension funds will be slightly higher than the 10% prescribed by law. See The World Bank, *Reforming the Pension Reforms: The Recent Initiatives and Actions on Pensions in Argentina and Chile*, SP Discussion Paper No. 0831, May 2008.

[11] International Social Security Association, http://www.issa.int/Observatory/Country-Profiles/Regions/Americas/ Chile/Scheme-Description/%28id%29/106103.

[12] A worker receives a total disability pension if he or she has lost at least 2/3 of ability to work. A worker receives a partial disability pension if he or she has lost between half and two-thirds of ability to work.

[13] Widows are allowed to receive both a survivor pension and a pension from their own individual account.

[14] The employer-provided voluntary savings plans, which were part of the 2008 reform package, resemble 401(k) defined contribution plans in the United States. Chilean employers can contract with any financial institution (AFP, banks, mutual funds or insurance companies) to establish a plan. Conditions must be the same for all workers and employers cannot under any circumstance restrict participation to certain groups of employees. See The World Bank, *Reforming the Pension Reforms: The Recent Initiatives and Actions on Pensions in Argentina and Chile*, SP Discussion Paper No. 0831, May 2008.

[15] If an AFP becomes insolvent, the Chilean government would provide a life annuity up to 100% of the minimum pension and 75% of the excess over and above that, up to a threshold.

[16] Superintendent of Pensions, Santiago, Chile, *The Chilean Pension System, Fourth Edition*, p. 47, at http://www.safp.cl/573/article-3523.html.

[17] Recognition bonds are issued to workers under the pay-as-you-go system who elected to switch to the individual account system starting in 1981. Recognition bonds are calculated as the capital needed to purchase a life annuity based on the worker's life expectancy and his or her contributions under the pay-as-you-go system, with some adjustments. Recognition bonds are financed out of general revenues and are redeemed when the worker reaches normal retirement age, becomes permanently disabled, or dies.

[18] The World Bank, *Reforming the Pension Reforms: The Recent Initiatives and Actions on Pensions in Argentina and Chile*, SP Discussion Paper No. 0831, May 2008, p. 45.

[19] The World Bank, *Reforming the Pension Reforms: The Recent Initiatives and Actions on Pensions in Argentina and Chile*, SP Discussion Paper No. 0831, May 2008, p. 48.

[20] The 1980 pension reform wrote most of these investment limits into the law. The 2008 reform package maintained over-arching limitations but transferred most of the regulatory authority for specific limits to Chilean government agencies (Central Bank and Superintendent of Pensions).

[21] Mauricio Soto, *Chilean Pension Reform: the Good, the Bad, and the In Between*, Center for Retirement Research at Boston College, IB no. 31, 2005, p. 3, http://crr.bc.edu/images. Participation is defined as contributing, in any month in 2003, to either an individual

account, the pre-1980 pay-as-you-go system, or one of the separate pension programs for certain groups of employees, such as public-sector workers, the military, and police.

[22] The extended coverage applies to all self-employed workers with income subject to the income tax. The most informal sectors of the economy, such as agricultural workers and small-scale producers and retailers, will not be brought into the pension system by the 2008 reforms.

[23] In 2003, for example, administrative costs and premiums averaged about 2.26% per month, of which about 1.51% was for administrative costs and about 0.75% was for survivor and disability insurance premiums. See CRS Report RL34006, *Social Security: The Chilean Approach to Retirement*, by Christopher Tamborini.

[24] As a result of the 2008 reforms, AFPs can only charge a single commission, which is expressed as a percentage of individual account earnings.

[25] Superintendent of Pensions, Santiago, Chile, Comunicado de Prensa, January 30, 2012, at http://www.spensiones.cl/ 573/article-7895.html.

[26] Stephen J. Kay, *The Perils of Private Pensions*, Foreign Policy, winter 1999-2000.

[27] Mauricio Soto, *Chilean Pension Reform: The Good, the Bad, and the In Between*, Center for Retirement Research at Boston College, Number 31, June 2005, at http://crr.bc.edu/briefs/chilean-pension-reform-

[28] The World Bank, Reforming *the Pension Reforms: The Recent Initiatives and Actions on Pensions in Argentina and Chile*, SP Discussion Paper No. 0831, May 2008, p. 57.

In: Chile
Editor: Garrett M. Ulrich

ISBN: 978-1-61122-031-5


*Chapter 3*

# CHILE 2013 HUMAN RIGHTS REPORT*

***U.S. Department of State; Bureau of Democracy, Human Rights and Labor***

## EXECUTIVE SUMMARY

Chile is a constitutional multi-party democracy. On December 15, in a presidential run-off following congressional, regional council, and a first round of presidential elections on November 17, Chileans elected former president Michelle Bachelet as their next president. All of the elections were considered to be free and fair. The new government will take office in March 2014. Authorities generally maintained effective control over the security forces. Security forces occasionally committed human rights abuses.

The principal human rights problems concerned discrimination against indigenous populations; societal violence and discrimination against women, children, and lesbian, gay, bisexual, and transgender (LGBT) persons; child labor; and harsh prison conditions and treatment.

Additional human rights concerns in the country included use of excessive force and abuse by security forces, isolated reports of government corruption, and anti-Semitism.

---

* This is an edited, reformatted and augmented version of a report released by the U.S. Department of State; Bureau of Democracy, Human Rights and Labor, dated February 2014.

The government generally took steps to prosecute officials who committed abuses. Nevertheless, many human rights organizations contended that security officials accused of committing abuses have impunity.

## Section 1. Respect for the Integrity of the Person, Including Freedom from

### *a. Arbitrary or Unlawful Deprivation of Life*

There were no reports that the government or its agents committed arbitrary or unlawful killings during the year. The external mechanism to investigate abuses by Carabineros is the military justice system, while the regular criminal justice system investigates accusations of abuse by investigative police (PDI) officers.

On January 3, authorities arrested six of eight former army officers indicted for the 1973 torture and subsequent execution of singer Victor Jara in the Estadio Chile in Santiago. On March 28, the Santiago Appellate Court approved bail for four of the eight. On October 11, the judge indicted and arrested a ninth former army officer. The case remained pending at year's end.

In June 2012 the Santiago Appellate Court ruled that Judge Mario Carroza should investigate the killing of U.S. citizen Ronnie Moffit in a Washington, D.C. car bombing in 1976. The case was pending at year's end.

According to the Diego Portales University (UDP) Law School's 2013 annual report on human rights, as of July the Supreme Court had ruled in 153 criminal cases of dictatorship-era human rights violations and confirmed 140 convictions, while 1,350 cases against more than 800 perpetrators remained under investigation or pending in the courts.

On March 25, a military prosecutor indicted former Carabinero sergeant Miguel Millacura for using unnecessary force and Lieutenant Claudia Iglesias for complicity in covering up Carabinero involvement in the 2011 killing of 16-year-old Manuel Gutierrez. Millacura was free on bail, and Iglesias reportedly continued on active duty. The status of the case in the military justice system against Millacura was unknown at year's end. Cases involving alleged unlawful conduct by Carabineros, including human rights abuses against civilians, were generally tried in the military court system, as were allegations where the accused is a member of the armed forces.

### *b. Disappearance*

There were no reports of politically motivated disappearances.

In August 2012 Judge Jorge Zepeda indicted eight former Carabineros and army patrol members for aggravated kidnapping in the 1985 disappearance case of U.S. citizen Boris Weisfeiler. The case remained pending at year's end; those charged remained free on bail.

### *c. Torture and Other Cruel, Inhuman, or Degrading Treatment or Punishment*

Although the constitution prohibits such practices, credible nongovernmental organizations (NGOs) received multiple reports of excessive force, abuse, and degrading treatment by Carabineros, PDI members, and prison guards, few of which resulted in convictions.

On June 13, Carabineros entered the downtown central campus of the University of Chile, allegedly without authorization and in a violent manner, in search of connections to several violent activities that took place the day before during an authorized student protest. According to local press, police seriously injured two female students resisting the unauthorized entrance. The head of the police unit involved was transferred to another unit after an internal investigation revealed a violation of protocol regarding the use of force. No further disciplinary action was taken.

On December 30, PDI officer Flavio Torres was charged in a Santiago court for unlawful coercion and computer crimes for his alleged role in the beating during the interrogation of a minor following a student protest in May. Torres was accused of participating in a group of approximately 10 officers who struck the minor's neck and face, photographed him in his underwear, and forced him to reveal his Facebook log-in credentials. The prosecutor said she was unable to determine the identities of others alleged to have been involved due to the invocation by the PDI of a provision of the country's National Intelligence Law. The judge, who remanded Torres into custody during the case's investigative phase, called the alleged crimes "among the most serious" contemplated by Chile's laws because they involved a state agent. The case was pending at year's end.

The National Institute of Human Rights (INDH) and media outlets reported on the alleged inappropriate use of force by prison guards in breaking up a protest at a prison in Valdivia in January, resulting in injuries to 21 inmates. The Court of Appeals of Valdivia subsequently made a special order of protection on behalf of the inmates. The Court of Appeals of Antofagasta ruled that prison guards violated constitutional rights of 10 inmates and breached the Convention Against Torture and Other Cruel, Inhuman or Degrading Treatment or Punishment during a violent encounter in July when the guards beat and shot pellets at prisoners, resulting in injuries.

**Prison and Detention Center Conditions**

Prison conditions were harsh. Human rights organizations reported that violence, including torture, occurred and that prison officials were aware of the problem and worked to address it. Violence among inmates was also common.

*Physical Conditions:* Prisons were overcrowded. The government reported that at the end of September, 45,510 prisoners were in prisons designed to hold 41,034 inmates. Prisoners included 3,540 women (held in separate sections of the same facilities as men or in separate facilities). At the end of August, 3,054 minors were in prisons or detention centers (held separately from the adult population). Many prisons were antiquated and offered substandard sanitary conditions, inadequate food, and insufficient medical services. Inadequate heating in some prisons remained a serious problem, and inadequate lighting and ventilation also affected inmates at some prisons. The government reported that access to potable water was limited in several prisons.

Officials reported 186 prisoner deaths during the year. Violence among inmates accounted for 67 deaths, while three inmates died while attempting to escape prison. On August 13, a fire broke out in a prison in Quillota, located near the coastal city of Valparaiso, after two rival gangs started a fight. Although the fire was contained, approximately 24 inmates were injured in the incident, five due to stab wounds that occurred during the intergang violence.

Prisoners with HIV/AIDS and mental and physical disabilities reportedly failed to receive adequate medical attention in some prisons. Adequate accommodations for those prisoners with physical disabilities were made.

According to the rights organization Movement for Homosexual Integration and Liberation (MOVILH) and various media outlets, in November 2012 an official commission reported that in a number of prisons, LGBT prisoners were separated from the general population to prevent possible attacks. The commission noted that that these separate facilities were overcrowded and lacked adequate basic hygienic services.

*Administration:* Recordkeeping on prisoners was generally adequate, and authorities used alternative sentencing for nonviolent offenders, such as conditional release for community service. There were no prison ombudsmen.

Prisoners and detainees had reasonable access to visitors and could observe their religious practices. Authorities permitted prisoners and detainees to submit complaints to judicial authorities without censorship and to request investigation of inhumane conditions. Authorities generally investigated credible allegations and documented the results in a publicly accessible manner. The government usually investigated and monitored prison and detention center conditions.

*Independent Monitoring:* The government permitted prison visits by independent human rights observers, and such visits took place at both government and privately operated facilities. Prisoner and human rights groups continued to investigate alleged use of abuse or excessive force against detainees, while the media covered some such allegations.

*Improvements:* Overcrowding decreased by almost 25 percent as of the end of September, compared with levels at the end of 2012. The government transferred inmates between prisons and issued pardons to certain inmates to reduce overcrowding. Two prisons were completely renovated, while several others underwent repairs and upgrades. Improved health measures were also implemented, including increased spending on meals. Nutritionists were hired to advise on healthy meal plans, leading to new nutrition programs in all prisons. The Human Rights division of the Gendarmeria held human rights-focused workshops, seminars, and other training programs at various prisons for current and future prison guards. The government also carried out an exhaustive survey of inmates from 75 prisons throughout the country for the purpose of understanding prisoners' perceptions of shortcomings in the penitentiary system, with the ultimate goal of improving the quality of life for prisoners. Based on those results, the Gendarmaria's human rights division planned to create a subdivision to monitor progress in efforts to address deficiencies and promote training of prison system personnel.

Gendarmeria officials participated in two educational sessions organized by NGOs aimed at instilling in prison employees respect for diversity and skills for handling LGBT-related issues in prisons. The Gendarmeria and MOVILH signed an agreement in December to facilitate the voluntary work of certain prisoners for MOVILH, with the aim of enhancing the quality of life for LGBT prisoners by increasing tolerance in more of the general prison population through education and exposure to LGBT-related matters.

The National Institute of Human Rights noted marked improvement in overall prison conditions.

### *d. Arbitrary Arrest or Detention*

The constitution prohibits arbitrary arrest and detention, and the government generally observed these prohibitions.

## Role of the Police and Security Apparatus

The Carabineros and the PDI have responsibility in law and practice for law enforcement and maintenance of order within the country. The Ministry of the Interior oversees both forces.

Civilian authorities generally maintained effective control over the Carabineros and the PDI, and the government has mechanisms to investigate and punish abuse and corruption. There were allegations of impunity involving security forces during the year. Cases from prior years remained pending in courts, while rights organizations criticized the security apparatus for failing to carry out sufficient internal reviews of allegations of abuse by their members and to take forceful enough action where wrongdoing was established. The 2012 Human Rights Watch country report noted continued concern that military courts were not fully independent and that investigations and trials of police accused of abuses against civilians continued to be conducted under the military justice system.

The external mechanism to investigate abuses by Carabineros is the military justice system, while accusations of abuses by PDI officers are investigated in the regular criminal justice system. The INDH stated in its 2013 annual report that there were 1,775 complaints against Carabineros in 2012 for "unnecessary violence" but that less than 2 percent of that number ended in convictions in the military justice system during the period. Carabineros accused of use of "unnecessary violence" are often re-assigned within the institution where an internal investigation reveals wrongdoing. The INDH reported that government actions to reform the security forces were lacking.

## Arrest Procedures and Treatment of Detainees

Only public officials expressly authorized by law can arrest or detain citizens and generally did so openly with warrants based on sufficient evidence brought before an independent judiciary. Authorities must immediately inform a prosecutor of an arrest and generally did so.

The prosecutor must open an investigation, receive a statement from the detainee, and ensure that the detainee is held at a local police station until the detention control hearing. Detention control hearings are held twice daily, allowing for a judicial determination of the legality of the detention within 24 hours of arrest. Detainees must be informed of their rights, including the right to an attorney and the right to remain silent until an attorney is present. Public defenders are provided to detainees who do not hire their own lawyer. Authorities must expedite notification of the detention to family members. If authorities do not inform the detainees of their rights upon detention, during the detention control hearing the judge can declare the process unlawful.

The law allows judges to set bail, grant provisional liberty, or order continued detention as necessary for the investigation or the protection of the prisoner or the public.

The law affords detainees 30 minutes of immediate and subsequent daily access to a lawyer (in the presence of a prison guard) and to a doctor to verify their physical condition. Regular visits by family members are allowed.

*Pretrial Detention:* Through September an average of 150 days passed between the time of arrest and presentation of charges against persons accused of a crime.

### *e. Denial of Fair Public Trial*

The constitution provides for an independent judiciary, and the government generally respected judicial independence.

### Trial Procedures

The constitution and law provide for the right to a fair trial, and an independent judiciary generally enforced this right.

Defendants enjoy a presumption of innocence and have a right of appeal. They have the right to be informed promptly of charges, have time to prepare their defense, and not be compelled to testify. The law provides for the right to a fair trial, and an independent judiciary generally enforced this right. National and regional prosecutors investigate crimes, formulate charges, and prosecute cases. Three-judge panels form the court of first instance. The process is oral and adversarial; trials are public; defendants have the right to be present and consult with an attorney in a timely manner; and judges rule on guilt and dictate sentences. Defendants do not enjoy the right to a trial by jury. Court records, rulings, and findings were generally accessible to the public.

The law provides for the right to legal counsel, and public defenders' offices across the country provided professional legal counsel to anyone seeking such assistance. When human rights organizations or family members requested, the NGO Corporation for the Promotion and Defense of the Rights of the People and other lawyers working pro bono assisted detainees during interrogation and trial. Defendants can confront or question adverse witnesses and present witnesses and evidence on their behalf, although the law provides for secret witnesses in certain circumstances. Defendants and their attorneys generally have access to government-held evidence relevant to their cases.

For crimes committed prior to the implementation of the 2005 judicial reforms, criminal proceedings are inquisitorial rather than adversarial. At year's end one inquisitorial criminal court remained open and had an extensive wait for trials.

**Political Prisoners and Detainees**

There were no reports of political prisoners or detainees, although some indigenous Mapuche convicted of criminal offenses claimed to be political prisoners.

**Civil Judicial Procedures and Remedies**

There is an independent and impartial judiciary in civil matters, which permits individuals to seek civil remedies for human rights violations; however, the civil justice system retained antiquated and inefficient procedures. The average civil trial lasted approximately five years, and civil suits could continue for decades. Administrative and judicial remedies are available for alleged wrongs. Cases involving violations of an individual's human rights may be submitted through petitions by individuals or organizations to the Inter-American Commission of Human Rights (IACHR), which in turn may submit the case to the Inter-American Court of Human Rights. The court can order civil remedies including fair compensation to the individual injured.

**Regional Human Rights Court Decisions**

Chile is subject to the jurisdiction of the Inter-American Court for Human Rights. On August 28, the court determined that the government was guilty of "undue delay" in investigating the exoneration claim of Leopoldo Garcia, who was tortured and exiled under the Pinochet government and submitted his request in 1993. The court ordered Chile to pay $32,000 in moral damages and to complete his investigation in a reasonable time. This was the first time the court ruled on a case involving the living survivor of human rights abuses from the Pinochet era.

### *f. Arbitrary Interference with Privacy, Family, Home, or Correspondence*

The constitution prohibits such actions, and the government generally respected these prohibitions.

## Section 2. Respect for Civil Liberties, Including

### *a. Freedom of Speech and Press*

The constitution provides for freedom of speech and press, and the government generally respected these rights. An independent press, an effective judiciary, and a functioning democratic political system combined to promote freedom of speech and of the press.

*Press Freedoms:* Although the independent media were active and expressed a wide variety of views without restriction, a 2013 Equitas Foundation report and a 2012 Freedom House report expressed concern with media concentration, whereby most media outlets are in the hands of two major family companies, Copesa and El Mercurio, which are the sole recipients of government subsidies. No legal framework exists to guarantee fair distributions of frequencies to different broadcast media.

*Libel Laws/National Security:* The penal code carries criminal sentences of six months to five years in jail for libel or slander. Press freedom groups called on the government to modify antiterrorism laws to limit their use on Chilean and foreign reporters, for example, on those who covered issues concerning Mapuche communities.

### Internet Freedom

There were no government restrictions on access to the internet or credible reports that the government monitored e-mail or internet chat rooms without appropriate legal authority. According to the International Telecommunication Union, approximately 41 percent of households had access to the internet in 2012.

### Academic Freedom and Cultural Events

There were no government restrictions on academic freedom or cultural events.

### *b. Freedom of Peaceful Assembly and Association*

#### Freedom of Assembly

The government routinely granted permits for marches and demonstrations, occasionally refusing permission for certain routes, citing a concern for public safety. Police used tear gas and water cannons and forcibly removed or detained some protesters when participants vandalized property.

#### Freedom of Association

The constitution provides for freedom of association, and the government generally respected this right.

### *c. Freedom of Religion*

See the Department of State's *International Religious Freedom Report* at www.state.gov/j/drl/irf/rpt/.

### *d. Freedom of Movement, Internally Displaced Persons, Protection of Refugees, and Stateless Persons*

The constitution provides for freedom of internal movement, foreign travel, emigration, and repatriation, and the government generally respected these rights.

The government cooperated with the Office of the UN High Commissioner for Refugees and other humanitarian organizations in providing protection and assistance to internally displaced persons, refugees, returning refugees, asylum seekers, stateless persons, and other persons of concern.

#### Protection of Refugees

*Access to Asylum:* The law provides for the granting of asylum or refugee status, and the government has established a system for providing protection to refugees.

During the first nine months of the year, six individuals received recognized refugee status, bringing the total number of refugees living in the country to 1,722.

## Section 3. Respect for Political Rights: The Right of Citizens to Change Their Government

The law provides citizens the right to change their government peacefully, and citizens exercised this right through periodic, free, and fair elections based on universal suffrage.

### *Elections and Political Participation*

*Recent Elections:* On December 15, Michele Bachelet was elected president in a free and fair run-off election. On November 17, in elections generally considered free and fair, voters elected 20 of 38 senators and all members of the Chamber of Deputies. A first-round presidential election took place the same day, but no candidate received more than the required 50 percent to win in the first round. For the first time since a June reform law, regional counselors were also elected nationwide. Newly elected officials are to take office in March 2014. In October 2012 mayors and city council members were elected nationwide in free and fair elections, the first following a 2011 change in election laws making voter registration automatic and voting voluntary.

*Participation of Women and Minorities:* There were 17 women in the 120-seat Chamber of Deputies and five women in the 38-seat Senate. There were six women in the 21-member cabinet. Indigenous people were active at the municipal level. Social, institutional, and cultural barriers limited indigenous participation in national elections, however.

## Section 4. Corruption and Lack of Transparency in Government

The law provides criminal penalties for corruption by officials, and the government generally implemented these laws effectively. There were isolated reports of government corruption during the year, which was more prevalent at the local level than the national level.

### *Corruption*

On July 5, authorities disclosed that Carabineros deleted wire-tap logs planned for use as evidence in a 2012 case in which 10 PDI detectives were charged with detaining suspects, giving false testimony, drug trafficking, and extortion. The National Prosecutor's Office began an immediate investigation, which delayed proceedings in the 2012 case against the Carabineros.

On September 5, after a three-year investigation, a court convicted the mayor of Hualpen of tax fraud and bribery and sentenced him to three years' probation, during which he cannot hold public office.

On November 25, four members of the Carabineros were arrested for alleged ties to drug trafficking. In response, the Carabineros named a new counternarcotics chief and announced a plan to restructure the counternarcotics department.

The Transparency Council is an autonomous government entity functioning to promote transparency in the public sector, monitor compliance, publish information on public offices, and guarantee access to information. The institution collaborated with civil society, operated effectively and independently, and had sufficient resources. It regularly published statistics on government compliance with the 2009 transparency law.

***Whistleblower Protection***

The law provides protection to public and private employees for making disclosures of illegality through the National Public Defender's Office or the local police. Few cases have been brought under the law

***Financial Disclosure***

A regulation subjects public officials to financial disclosure and assigns responsibility to the comptroller for conducting audits of government agencies and to the Public Prosecutor's Office for initiating criminal investigations of official corruption. The law requires that all declarations be made public, provides sanctions for noncompliance, and clearly identifies which assets must be declared; however, it does not mandate a unit to monitor disclosures.

***Public Access to Information***

The constitution requires the government and its agencies to make all unclassified information about their activities available to the public. The government granted citizens and noncitizens, including foreign media, access to all unclassified information. The law regulates government transparency and provides public access to information. The law applies to ministries; regional, provincial, and municipal level governments; the armed forces, police, and public security forces; and public enterprises where the state owns more than 50 percent or holds a majority of appointments on the board of directors. The law has a list of five exceptions for nondisclosure. Responses to any requests for information must be delivered within 20 business days, and there is no cost for the request. In cases of noncompliance, the head of the organization is subject to a fine between 20 percent and 50 percent of his or her monthly salary. The autonomous Transparency Council provides for the right of access to information and issues rulings on cases in which information is denied.

## Section 5. Governmental Attitude Regarding International and Nongovernmental Investigation of Alleged Violations of Human Rights

A number of domestic and international human rights groups generally operated without government restriction, investigating and publishing their findings on human rights cases. Government officials were generally cooperative and responsive to their views, although some indigenous rights groups claimed their views were disregarded.

***Government Human Rights Bodies***

The INDH, an autonomous government entity, operated independently, issued public statements, and proposed changes to government agencies or policies to promote and protect human rights. INDH's 2013 annual report noted concern over several human rights problems, including access to justice; excessive police force; violence against women and children; societal abuses against youth, immigrants, transgender persons, and other minorities; and the continued application of the antiterrorism law, including in cases involving members of indigenous communities. The Senate and Chamber of Deputies also have standing human rights committees responsible for drafting human rights legislation.

## Section 6. Discrimination, Societal Abuses, and Trafficking in Persons

The constitution states the all persons are born free and are equal in terms of the law and dignity; however, it does not specifically identify groups protected from discrimination. The 2012 Anti-Discrimination Law provides civil legal remedies to victims of discrimination based on race, ethnicity, nationality, socioeconomic situation, language, ideology or political opinion, religion or belief, association or participation in union organizations or lack thereof, gender, sexual orientation, gender identification, marriage status, age, affiliation, personal appearance, and sickness or physical disability. The law also increases criminal penalties for acts of violence based on discrimination, but such discrimination continued to occur.

### *Women*

#### Rape and Domestic Violence

The law criminalizes rape, including spousal rape. Penalties for rape range from five to 15 years' imprisonment, and the government generally enforced the law when violations were reported.

The law protects the privacy and safety of the victim making the charge. Between January and November, the Public Prosecutor's Office investigated 4,676 cases of rape, and the courts handed down 469 rape convictions and convicted 431 individuals between January and November. Experts, however, believed that most rape cases went unreported due to fear of further violence, retribution, and social stigma.

The law criminalizes both physical and psychological domestic violence. Nevertheless, it remained a serious problem in the country. From January to June, police filed 66,523 cases of domestic violence. From January to September, there were 32,638 convictions and 140 sentences. Family courts handle cases of domestic violence and penalize offenders with fines up to 556,680 pesos ($1,145). Additional sanctions include eviction of the offender from the residence shared with the victim, restraining orders, confiscation of firearms, and court-ordered counseling. Cases of habitual psychological abuse and physical abuse cases in which there are physical injuries are prosecuted in the criminal justice system. Penalties are based on the gravity of injuries and range from 61 to 540 days' imprisonment.

Authorities generally enforced the law in cases reported to them, and there was no indication of police or judicial reluctance to act. Experts believed that most domestic violence cases went unreported due to fear of further violence, retribution, and social stigma. The *National Survey of Domestic Violence 2012* revealed that 32 percent of women suffered some kind of domestic violence from their family members, partners, or former partners during their lifetime. Of these aggressions, women reported only 36 percent to authorities, citing fear as the main reason for not reporting.

In its 2012 country report, the UN Convention on the Elimination of All Forms of Discrimination against Women (CEDAW) expressed concern at the lack of measures taken by the government to address other forms of violence against women, including femicide outside the family sphere and sexual violence. CEDAW also expressed concern at the disproportionate use of violence by police, including sexual abuse against female students during social protests and against women during Mapuche protests, an absence of prosecution of perpetrators, and the government's failure to provide access to justice to women victims of such violence.

The government added social media to the domestic violence media campaign launched in 2010. The National Women's Service (SERNAM) operated 96 assistance centers or "Women's Centers" and 23 women's shelters, and it maintained partnerships with NGOs to provide training sessions for police officers and judicial and municipal authorities on the legal and psychological aspects of domestic violence. The Ministry of Justice and the PDI operated several offices specifically dedicated to providing counseling and assistance in rape cases. SERNAM also operated a 24-hour hotline for victims of violence, including domestic abuse and rape. In October SERNAM launched a new awareness campaign, "Violence Against Women Angers Me," to address this abuse. Data was not available to assess the effectiveness of government campaigns against domestic and sexual violence.

**Sexual Harassment**

Sexual harassment is not a criminal offense but is classified as a misdemeanor, with penalties outlined exclusively in the labor code. By law, sexual harassment is cause for immediate dismissal from employment. The law requires employers to define internal procedures for investigating sexual harassment, and employers may face fines and additional financial compensation to victims if internal procedures are not met. The law provides protection to victims of sexual harassment by employers and coworkers. It also provides severance pay to victims who resign due to sexual harassment if they have completed at least one year with the employer. Authorities generally enforced the law in cases reported to them, and there was no evidence of police or judicial reluctance to act. From January to August, the Labor Directorate received 111 complaints of sexual harassment reported by individuals and companies, and companies were sanctioned for procedural noncompliance.

**Reproductive Rights**

Couples and individuals had the right to decide freely and responsibly the number, spacing, and timing of their children and had the information and means to do so free from discrimination, coercion, and violence. Government policy did not interfere with access to contraception, skilled attendance during childbirth, prenatal care, or essential obstetric and postpartum care. Despite the fact that emergency contraception is legal and that the law provides for the free distribution of emergency contraception in the public health system, many hospitals and clinics continued to refuse to prescribe it.

**Discrimination**

Although women possess most of the same legal rights as men, discrimination in employment, pay, owning and managing businesses, and education persisted. There were no known reports of discrimination in credit or housing. The default and most common marital arrangement is "conjugal society," which gives a husband the right to administer joint property, including his wife's property. As a result, women who were married under the conjugal society arrangement were usually required to obtain permission from their husbands to apply for housing subsidies and take out loans or mortgages, while men had unrestricted access to these and other services. Legislation remained pending six years after a 2007 agreement with the IACHR to modify the "conjugal society law" to give women and men equal rights and responsibilities in marriage. The commercial code provides that, unless a woman is married under the separate estate regime, she may not enter into a commercial partnership agreement without permission from her husband, while a man may enter into such an agreement without permission from his wife.

Despite a law providing for equal pay for equal work, the average woman's annual income was 49 percent that of men, according to the World Economic Forum's *2013 Global Gender Gap Report*. Fifty-two percent of women participated in the labor force during the year (compared with 79 percent of men), but 74 percent of women enrolled in tertiary education, compared with 67 percent of men. SERNAM is in charge of protecting women's legal rights and is the only government office that deals specifically with discrimination against women. There are 96 "women's centers" throughout the country to help establish equal rights for women by offering services such as training, counseling, and legal advice.

*Children*

**Birth Registration**

Citizenship is derived by birth within the country's territory and from one's parents or grandparents. Births are registered immediately.

**Child Abuse**

Violence against children remained a significant problem. From January to September, the Public Prosecutor's Office initiated investigations into 17,636 cases of child sexual abuse, some including domestic violence. The trial of Juan Romeo Gomez, a schoolteacher indicted in 2012 for 77 cases of sexual abuse of children, remained in progress in November.

The National Children's Service (SENAME) reported 9,220 cases of sex abuse of children under age 14. A 2012 law makes those convicted of child sexual abuse permanently ineligible for any position, job, career, or profession in educational settings requiring direct and habitual contact with children under age 18. This law also includes a public registry of these sex offenders. Educational and other establishments that work with children are obligated to consult the registry as part of the hiring process.

In July national and international media reported the case of an 11-year-old girl who was raped and impregnated by her mother's partner. At year's end the accused was in pretrial detention while a criminal case continued. SENAME also launched a protective case in family court on behalf of the girl, who was living with other family members.

On December 31, two former school employees were sentenced to 10 and 15 years in prison for rape and sexual abuse towards three students from 2012.

**Forced and Early Marriage**

The legal minimum age of marriage is 18 (16 with parental consent). According to the National Statistics Institute, 0.7 percent of females and 2.9 percent of males between the ages of 15 and 19 got married in 2011. There were no reported cases of marriage under the age of 15.

**Sexual Exploitation of Children**

The penalties for commercial sexual exploitation of children range from three to five years in prison. The range increases from five years and a day to 20 years and a fine of 31 to 35 UTM or 1.264 million pesos to 1.427 million pesos ($2,400 to $2,715) in cases where exploitation is habitual, or if there was deceit or abuse of authority or trust. (The monthly tax unit, or UTM, is a legally defined currency unit, indexed to inflation, equivalent to 40,772 pesos ($78). The legal age for consensual sex is 18. Sex with a girl between ages 14 and 18 may be considered statutory rape, and sex with a child under age 14 is considered rape, regardless of consent or the victim's gender. Penalties for statutory rape range from five to 20 years in prison. Child pornography is a crime. Penalties for producing child pornography range from 541 days to five years in prison.

Commercial sexual exploitation of children and adolescents was a problem, and children were exploited in prostitution with and without third-party involvement. From January to September, the Public Prosecutor's Office initiated 186 investigations into commercial sexual exploitation of children, and the courts handed down 65 convictions. In 2012 SENAME, the Ministry of Justice, and civil society organizations launched a Second Plan of Action against the Commercial Sexual Exploitation of Children for 2012 to 2014.

**Institutionalized Children**

In June SENAME published a *Guide to Prevention of Sexual Abuse in Residences* and distributed copies to all residences.

**International Child Abductions**

The country is a party to the 1980 Hague Convention on the Civil Aspects of International Child Abduction. For more information see the Department of State's country-specific information at www.travel.state.gov/abduction/country/country_3781.html.

***Anti-Semitism***

The Jewish community numbered approximately 20,500. There were reports of societal abuses or discrimination based on religious affiliation, belief, or practice. Anti-Semitic incidents included verbal slurs, online harassment, and vandalism.

Authorities and Jewish community groups noted anti-Semitic comments, including via social media and e-mail correspondence.

On May 20, comedian Elias Escobedo on the national "Hazme Reir" television program made anti-Semitic jokes when referring to the Holocaust. The Jewish Community of Chile condemned the remarks, reported an increase in anti-Semitic e-mails received through its website, and noted anti-Semitic comments made to online articles published about the incident. In response the television station dismissed Escobedo, and the National Television Council fined the station.

***Trafficking in Persons***

See the Department of State's *Trafficking in Persons Report* at www.state.gov/j/tip/.

***Persons with Disabilities***

The law prohibits discrimination against persons with physical, sensory, intellectual, and mental disabilities in employment, education, air travel and other transportation, access to health care, and the provision of other state services, and the government effectively enforced these provisions. Nevertheless, persons with disabilities suffered forms of de facto discrimination. The law provides for universal and equal access to buildings, information, and communications. Most public buildings did not comply with legal accessibility mandates. The public transportation system, particularly outside Santiago, did not adequately provide accessibility for persons with disabilities. In recent years, however, TranSantiago, the main system of public transportation within Santiago, instituted changes to improve compliance with the law, including new ramp systems and elevators at certain metro stations.

The National Service for the Disabled (SENADIS) reported that children with disabilities attended school (primary and secondary) but noted that there were difficulties in ensuring these children received equal access to schooling at private institutions. SENADIS also reported that those with disabilities had fewer opportunities to continue with their education following secondary school. Persons with disabilities often faced discrimination in hiring; they constituted approximately 7.6 percent of the population but only 0.5 percent of the workforce. Although there is an active program, Sello Chile Inclusivo, to promote the integration of persons with disabilities into the workforce, its effectiveness was questioned due to reports of discrepancies in wages and benefits between those with and without disabilities in the same office and a lack of connections to small businesses.

SENADIS operates under the jurisdiction of the Ministry of Planning, has responsibility for protecting the rights of persons with disabilities, and advocates and promotes integration and protection policies throughout all government agencies. In preparation for the 2013 presidential and congressional elections, SENADIS published a guide outlining the rights when at the polls and voting for persons with disabilities. These rights include assistance gaining access to a ballot and in the polling booth, as needed. Persons with disabilities were provided assistance, as needed, at polling stations.

### *National/Racial/Ethnic Minorities*

On October 19, approximately 150 citizens of the northern city of Antofagasta protested against the presence of Colombians in their city, accusing the approximately 27,000 Colombians living legally in Antofagasta of taking jobs and bringing drugs into the city.

### *Indigenous People*

Indigenous people (approximately 5 percent of the total population) have the right to participate in decisions affecting their lands, cultures, and traditions, including the exploitation of energy, minerals, timber, or other natural resources on indigenous lands. Of the indigenous population, 80 percent belong to the Mapuche people. The 2013 INDH annual report noted again that, despite government policies designed to address the situation of social and political exclusion of indigenous peoples, systematic inequities persisted. Indigenous people also experienced societal discrimination, including in employment, and there were reports of incidents in which they were attacked and harassed. Indigenous women faced triple discrimination on the basis of their gender, indigenous background, and reduced economic status, and they were especially vulnerable to violence, poverty, and illness. The constitution does not specifically protect indigenous groups. The government's National Indigenous Development Corporation has an annual budget of 91.17 billion pesos ($200 million) to fund programs for indigenous communities.

Instances of violence between Mapuche and landowners, logging companies, and police in the southern part of the country continued throughout the year. The actions usually took the form of protests, including the use of violence, regarding historic Mapuche concerns about their rights to ancestral lands. Mapuche activists and police forces stationed in the area to guard private lands sometimes engaged in violent skirmishes. On January 3, several individuals allegedly linked to Mapuche activist groups set fire to the home of the Luchsinger-Mackay family in Vilcun, resulting in the death of two people. One Mapuche individual, Celestino Cordova, was arrested and charged under the antiterrorism law with the crime of terrorist arson. After four postponements, trial preparations began on October 22. Cordova remained in pretrial detention at year's end.

There were numerous reports of police abuse against Mapuche individuals and communities, including against children. In April PDI officers carried out aggressive raids in the Mapuche community of Freire in search of illegal arms. A case was subsequently brought in court against the officers due to the aggressive tactics used in the presence of a number of indigenous youth. In July the Appeals Court of Temuco ruled that the officers "infringed the right of personal liberty and individual security" in carrying out the raids.

The Equitas Foundation noted that sentences by the military justice system against police convicted of crimes against Mapuche were noticeably more lenient than sentences for Mapuche individuals. There was very little publicly available information on cases tried in the military system. This lack of transparency led to questions regarding justice for victims of abuse by police and military personnel.

The NGO Citizens' Observatory reported police searches of Mapuche homes without a warrant, arrest and release of Mapuche individuals without a detention control hearing, and police use of intimidation and discriminatory statements against Mapuche individuals, including minors.

In his July visit, the UN special rapporteur on counterterrorism and human rights found examples of legal discrimination against the Mapuche. He recommended that authorities adopt a comprehensive national strategy to address the Mapuche question, refrain from applying antiterrorism legislation in connection with Mapuche indigenous peoples' land protests, and end de facto impunity for crimes committed by law enforcement officials against members of the Mapuche community over the past decade. In August the UN Committee on the Elimination of Racial Discrimination recommended that the country quicken the process of returning lands to indigenous peoples throughout the country; improve indigenous consultation, particularly with respect to natural resource development; and clearly define crimes that fall under the antiterrorism law while ensuring the law is not used inappropriately against the Mapuche people. Both the 2013 UDP annual report on human rights and the 2013 INDH annual report also criticized the use of the antiterrorism law in the context of intercultural conflict.

On August 12, the Supreme Court reversed the August 2012 military court acquittal of special operations police corporal Miguel Patricio Jara for the use of unnecessary force resulting in the 2009 death of Mapuche protester Jaime Mendoza. A lower military court had convicted Jara in 2011. The Supreme Court sentenced Jara to three years but let him serve his sentence on parole.

The exploitation of energy, minerals, and timber occurred near indigenous communities, including mining projects in the northern regions where Aymara, Atacameno, and Diaguita peoples live, and timber exploitation in the south where the Mapuche live. Indigenous lands are effectively demarcated, but some indigenous Mapuche communities demanded restitution of privately and publicly owned traditional lands. Mining projects in the north generated judicial actions by indigenous communities due to concerns regarding potential contamination of the water supply and environment as well as project demands for water in desert environments. Timber plantations in the south also generated concerns regarding their effects on the water table due to the introduction of nonnative species. An INDH report released in May stated that negative externalities associated with the large-scale forestry industry affected 70 percent of Mapuche communities between Arauco to Chiloe in the southern area of the country.

On July 1, the courts rejected a Mapuche family's appeal objecting to a hydroelectric project in Futrono. Mapuche and NGO actors asserted that indigenous communities affected by the negative externalities associated with major development projects were not considered in the planning of such projects or in extending compensatory benefits. The 2013 INDH annual report and the 2013 UDP annual report on human rights emphasized the need to improve consultation mechanisms for indigenous peoples in the planning process of projects near indigenous communities.

***Societal Abuses, Discrimination, and Acts of Violence Based on Sexual Orientation and Gender Identity***

MOVILH reported 148 cases of discrimination due to sexual orientation and gender identity during the year, compared with 186 reported cases in 2011. MOVILH noted a worsening in the acts of violence against LGBT individuals between 2011 and 2012, including three killings, 20 acts of physical or verbal aggression, six incidents involving aggression and/or arbitrary police arrest, nine incidents of employment discrimination, 10 incidents of education discrimination, and 12 acts of violence or forced community segregation by family or friendship circles.

During the year there were a number of brutal attacks. On February 5, unknown assailants attacked Nicole Vicuna, a transgender female, while she was walking in Valparaiso; observers attributed the attack to Vicuna's sexual identity. Her attackers specifically targeted her face, and due to injuries, she lost sight in her right eye. According to the Organization for Transgender Dignity and Diversity, the Carabineros opened an investigation but did little to pursue the case.

Authorities also appeared reluctant to investigate and prosecute other cases, such as the June 23 attack on Esteban Navarro and the October 29 attack on Vladimir Supelveda, both of whom were assaulted due to their sexual orientation and suffered serious physical injuries.

On December 26, while walking down the street with friends in Santiago, Arturo Lomboi was verbally assaulted and fatally shot in an attack observers attributed to Lomboi's sexual orientation. Authorities issued a warrant for the arrest of the assailant, but by year's end, no arrest had been made.

On December 26, the Appellate Court upheld the convictions of four alleged neo-Nazis of first-degree murder in the 2012 torture and death of Daniel Zamudio because of his sexual orientation. The group leader, Patricio Ahumada, received life in prison; Alejandro Angulo and Raul Lopez both received 15 years; and the fourth member, Fabian Mora, received eight years since he first confessed to the attack. Laws prevent transgender persons from changing gender markers on government-issued identity documents, including national identity cards and university diplomas, to match their outward appearance or chosen expression. On May 22, Valentina Verbal, the country's first transgender congressional candidate, abandoned her campaign for the Chamber of Deputies after the Electoral Commission mandated that she use her birth gender and name on the official ballot instead of her gender-identified name of Valentina. Verbal filed a complaint with the IACHR, which was pending in November.

***Other Societal Violence or Discrimination***

Social and cultural barriers in terms of reproductive rights existed in some cases. The law on surgical sterilizations requires voluntary informed consent; however, in its 2012 report, CEDAW recognized continued cases of health-care workers pressuring or forcing HIV-positive women into surgical sterilization and urged the government to ensure that medical personnel seek fully informed consent before performing sterilizations and that those who perform unauthorized sterilization are sanctioned under the law.

Women faced significant obstacles to preventing HIV infection, including social and cultural norms; gender-based violence; and limited public-health awareness, outreach, and education. The law prohibits discrimination against persons on the basis of their HIV status, and in the area of health care, the law provides that neither public nor private health institutions can deny access to health-care services on the basis of a person's serological status. In 2012, however, CEDAW reported that HIV-positive women received discriminatory health-care treatment, especially in reproductive health services. Problems included delayed care, verbal abuse, pressure not to have children, and refusal of treatment. In 2012 the Ministry of Health launched a national campaign to encourage citizens to be tested for HIV.

## Section 7. Worker Rights

### *a. Freedom of Association and the Right to Collective Bargaining*

The law, including related regulations and statutory instruments, provides for the right of workers to form and join independent unions of their choice without previous authorization, with the exception of police and military personnel. Union leaders are restricted from being members of political parties, and the Directorate of Labor has broad powers to monitor unions' financial accounts and financial transactions.

With some limitations, the law also provides for the right to strike, protects the right of collective bargaining, and prohibits antiunion practices. The law prohibits public employees from striking. While employees in the private sector have the right to strike, the law places some restrictions on this right. For instance an absolute majority of workers must approve strikes. Strikes by agricultural workers during the harvest season are prohibited. The law also prohibits employees of 101 private-sector companies, largely providers of services such as water and electricity, from striking and stipulates compulsory arbitration to resolve disputes in these companies. The law does not specifically prohibit employers from dismissing striking workers, but employers must show cause and pay severance benefits if they dismiss strikers.

The law protects collective bargaining, with exceptions for some companies regulated in the labor code, such as public institutions, private and public institutions whose budget is dependent upon the Defense Ministry, companies that are unable to negotiate at certain times of the year, and companies in which employees are unable to strike, such as health care and public utilities. The law guarantees collective bargaining rights only at the company level. Collective bargaining in the agricultural sector remained dependent on employers' agreeing to negotiate, since most of these workers were temporary and not automatically eligible for collective bargaining. Intercompany unions are permitted to bargain collectively only when the individual employers all agree to negotiate under such terms.

The government generally enforced labor laws effectively. Nevertheless, the Labor Directorate under the Ministry of Labor commented on the need for more inspectors and noted that financial penalties did not always deter companies from repeating offenses. Companies are generally subject to sanctions for violations to the labor code of one to 10 UTM ($78 to $780) for micro and small businesses, two to 40 UTM ($144 to $2,880) for medium businesses and three to 60 UTM ($216 to $4,230) for large businesses according to the severity of each case. Companies may receive "special sanctions" for infractions such as causing irreversible injuries to an employee, antiunion practices or denying maternity leave. NGOs reported that cases in labor tribunals system took approximately three months. Cases regarding fundamental rights of the worker often took closer to six months. NGOs continued to report that it was difficult for judges to enforce decisions in favor of workers for various reasons, including when the company's assets were in a different name or juridical entity that could not be located.

Freedom of association was generally respected. Employers sometimes did not respect the right to collective bargaining. Between January and August, the Labor Directorate received 1,284 complaints of violations to collective-bargaining regulations. The government protected the right to strike. Despite being prohibited by law, public-sector and health-care worker strikes occurred throughout the year. Worker organizations operated independent of the government and political parties. According to Freedom House and the International Trade Union Confederation, antiunion practices, such as replacing workers on strike and illegal separation of union members, continued to occur. Both NGOs and unions reported companies also used sub- and temporary contracts as well as obtaining several fiscal registration/tax identification numbers as a form of antiunion discrimination and to increase the size of the workforce without granting collective bargaining rights.

***b. Prohibition of Forced or Compulsory Labor***

The law prohibits all forms of forced or compulsory labor. In general the government effectively enforced applicable laws. Penalties of five to 15 years for violations were sufficiently stringent to deter violations. In June the Labor Directorate together with the Public Prosecutor's Office and the Ministry of Interior held training for inspectors on identifying labor trafficking. Despite increases in the number of inspectors and improved training, finding and identifying both perpetrators and victims of forced labor continued to be a challenge.

Forced labor continued to occur. Foreign citizens, including men, women, and children, were subjected to forced labor in the mining, agriculture, domestic service, and hospitality sectors. Some children were forcibly employed in the drug trade (see 7. c.).

Also see the Department of State's *Trafficking in Persons Report* at www.state.gov/j/tip/.

workers at high altitudes, who may exchange a work-free day each week for several consecutive work-free days every two weeks. The law establishes fines for employers who compel workers to work in excess of 10 hours a day or do not provide adequate rest days. Annual leave for full-time workers is 15 workdays, and workers with more than 10 years of service are eligible for an additional day of annual leave for every three years worked. Overtime is considered to be any time worked beyond the 45-hour workweek, and workers are due time and a half pay for any overtime performed. The law sets fines for noncompliance with labor regulations.

The law establishes occupational safety and health standards, which are applicable to all sectors. Special safety and health norms exist for specific sectors, such as mining and diving. The National Service for Geology and Mines is further mandated to regulate and inspect the mining industry. The law does not regulate the informal sector.

The Labor Directorate under the Ministry of Labor is responsible for enforcing minimum wage and other labor laws and regulations, and it did so effectively in the formal economy. The Ministries of Health and Labor administered and effectively enforced occupational safety and health standards. Workers in the informal economy were not effectively protected in regards to wage or safety. Insurance mutual funds are private nonprofit institutions that receive a commission from the government to provide workers' compensation and occupational safety training for the private and public sectors.

The Labor Directorate employed 1,229 labor inspectors during the year. Both the Labor Directorate and NGOs reported the need for more inspectors to enforce labor laws throughout the country, particularly in remote areas. NGOs commented that inspectors and labor tribunal judges needed more training and that a lack of information and economic means generated an inequality between parties in cases before the tribunals. Fines were not considered to have a deterrent effect with larger employers. The Labor Directorate worked preventively with small and medium-sized businesses to assist in their compliance with labor laws.

Minimum wage violations were most common in the real estate and commerce sectors. A Ministry of Economy report published in April based upon 2011 statistics indicated that between 15 and 17 percent of the formal workforce received the minimum wage.

As of September the sectors with the most infractions in safety and health standards were construction, industrial manufacturing, and commerce. Between July 2012 and June 2013, 301 workplace fatalities and 199,325 workplace accidents were registered. The service sector suffered the most accidents during the year. Immigrant workers in the agricultural sector were the group most likely to be subject to exploitative working conditions.

In: Chile
Editor: Garrett M. Ulrich
ISBN: 978-1-61122-031-5


*Chapter 4*

# CHILE 2012 INTERNATIONAL RELIGIOUS FREEDOM REPORT*

*U.S. Department of State; Bureau of Democracy, Human Rights and Labor*

## EXECUTIVE SUMMARY

The constitution and other laws and policies protect religious freedom and, in practice, the government generally respected religious freedom. The trend in the government's respect for religious freedom did not change significantly during the year.

There were reports of societal abuses or discrimination based on religious affiliation, belief, or practice. Incidents of anti-Semitism included online harassment, verbal slurs, and increased vandalism.

U.S. embassy officials discussed religious tolerance with the National Office of Religious Affairs (ONAR) and leaders of numerous religious groups, focusing on the value of deepening institutional cooperation. The embassy organized an iftar with an ecumenical group of religious leaders, and embassy officers attended interfaith events.

* This is an edited, reformatted and augmented version of a report released by the U.S. Department of State; Bureau of Democracy, Human Rights and Labor, dated May 2013.

## Section I. Religious Demography

According to the 2012 census, the population is 16.6 million. Religious affiliation statistics from the 2012 census were not available at year's end. According to the 2002 census, 70 percent of the population over the age of 14 is Roman Catholic and 15 percent is "evangelical," a term referring to all non-Catholic Christian groups except The Church of Jesus Christ of Latter-day Saints (Mormons), Jehovah's Witnesses, Orthodox (Armenian, Greek, Persian, Serbian, and Ukrainian churches), and Seventh-day Adventist. Approximately 90 percent of "evangelicals" are Pentecostal. Anglican, Baptist, Episcopalian, Lutheran, Methodist, Presbyterian, Reformed Evangelical, and Wesleyan groups constitute the remaining 10 percent. Bahais, Buddhists, Jews, Muslims, and members of the Unification Church collectively constitute less than 5 percent of the population.

According to the 2002 census, 5 percent of the population self-identifies as "indigenous," of whom 65 percent identify as Catholic, 29 percent as Protestant, and 6 percent as "other."

## Section II. Status of Government Respect for Religious Freedom

### Legal/Policy Framework

The constitution and other laws and policies protect religious freedom.

Church and state are officially separate. The law prohibits religious discrimination. The ONAR is part of the executive branch and is responsible for promoting religious freedom and tolerance. The office's mandate is to work with all religious organizations to implement constitutional provisions on religious freedom.

The law allows any religious group to apply for religious nonprofit status. The Ministry of Justice may not refuse to accept a registration petition, although it may object to the petition within 90 days if all legal prerequisites for registration are not satisfied. The petitioner then has 60 days to address objections the ministry raises or challenge the ministry in court. Once registered, the state cannot dissolve a religious entity by decree. The semiautonomous Council for the Defense of the State may initiate a judicial review, but the government has never de-registered a legally registered group.

The law allows religious group to adopt a charter and bylaws suited to a religious group rather than a private corporation. Religious groups may establish affiliates (schools, clubs, and sports organizations) without registering them as separate entities. There are more than 2,700 registered religious groups.

An Anti-Discrimination Law approved on July 24 gives civil legal remedies to victims of various types of discrimination, including those based on religion or belief. The law also increases criminal penalties for acts of violence based on discrimination.

Publicly-subsidized schools must offer religious education for two teaching hours per week through high school. Parents may have their children excused from religious education. Local school administrators decide how funds are spent on religious instruction. The majority of religious instruction in public schools is Catholic, although the Ministry of Education has approved curricula for 14 other religious groups. Schools must teach the religion requested by the parents. Parents may homeschool their children for religious reasons or enroll them in private schools.

The law grants religious groups the right to have chaplains in public hospitals, prisons, and military units. Regulations for the armed forces and law enforcement agencies allow officially registered religious groups to appoint chaplains to serve in each branch of the armed forces, in the national uniformed police, and the national investigative police.

The ONAR trains clergy of various religions on hospital protocol and issues government identification badges. A new accreditation process implemented in June for representatives of all religions improves the access of hospital patients to their preferred religious representatives. The prison system has both Catholic and Protestant staff chaplains and a large number of volunteer chaplains. The government observes the following religious holidays as national holidays: Good Friday, the Feast of the Virgin of Carmen, the Feast of Saints Peter and Paul, the Feast of the Assumption, National Day of Evangelical Churches, All Saints' Day, the Feast of the Immaculate Conception, and Christmas.

## Government Practices

There were no reports of abuses of religious freedom.

Catholicism was the dominant religion in public schools, prisons, hospitals, and the military. Representatives from the ONAR held regular roundtable meetings with Protestant leaders to discuss mechanisms to increase Protestant pastoral presence in these institutions. Catholic chaplains outnumbered Protestant chaplains in all branches of the armed forces, and Protestant leaders continued to advocate for more paid chaplain positions.

The celebration of Catholic mass frequently marked official and public events. At military events, all members of participating units were obliged to attend. Government officials attended Catholic events, and major Protestant and Jewish ceremonies.

In October President Pinera announced the appointment of a rabbi as one of three chaplains serving La Moneda Palace, joining the Catholic and Protestant chaplains there. He also thanked the Jewish community for its many contributions to Chilean society. Members of the Jewish Community of Chile (CJCH) told the press the appointment reflected the country's movement toward greater tolerance and diversity.

Enforcement of the requirement to provide non-Catholic education when parents requested it was weak. As part of a two-phase program, ONAR officials traveled to various regions and met with educators and religious leaders to stress that non-Catholic religion classes, specifically Protestant classes, must be offered when requested. The ONAR also provided assistance to municipal offices of religious affairs to develop community-supported curricula in public schools.

## SECTION III. STATUS OF SOCIETAL RESPECT FOR RELIGIOUS FREEDOM

There were reports of societal abuses or discrimination based on religious affiliation, belief, or practice. Anti-Semitic incidents included verbal slurs, online harassment, and an increase in vandalism. Jewish government officials reported receiving anti-Semitic correspondence. Authorities and Jewish community groups noted an increase in anti-Semitic comments, including via social media.

Street protests over education and other social issues led to increased levels of graffiti including swastikas and other expressions of anti-Semitism in major cities. In January anti-Semitic comments in social media spiked following claims that an Israeli tourist had started a forest fire. Protests in response to events in the Middle East, which normally took place at the Israeli embassy, expanded to the CJCH Center. On January 21, three youths beat and verbally harassed a 23-year-old Jewish man at a party in Ritoque. Others at the party refused to assist the victim or to transport him to the hospital. The CJCH condemned the act.

On August 19, a neo-Nazi group in the Araucania Region attacked a 14-year-old boy and drew a swastika on his stomach with a syringe. In September, coinciding with the Jewish holidays of Yom Kippur and Rosh Hashanah, the CJCH in Santiago reported that vandals marked synagogues and schools with swastikas and the phrase "Juden raus," meaning "Jews out." The Jewish community noted an increase in anti-Semitism throughout the year and leaders took precautions to ensure their safety.

On August 24, the president of the Palestinian Federation of South America, which represented more than 300,000 Chileans of Palestinian descent, made anti-Semitic remarks to the media, comparing Zionists to Nazis. Neo-Nazi and skinhead groups engaged in gang-type criminal activities and anti-Semitic rhetoric.

## SECTION IV. U.S. GOVERNMENT POLICY

U.S. embassy representatives met periodically with religious leaders and ONAR officials. Discussions focused on the value of deepening institutional cooperation and the importance of passing the new antidiscrimination law, a theme many Jewish leaders emphasized.

On July 26, the deputy chief of mission hosted an iftar to promote religious tolerance. Forty-four leaders of various religious groups and representatives of other embassies attended. The event emphasized religious tolerance and the role of interfaith dialogue, and honored the Muslim tradition of iftar in a religiously diverse setting.

On November 9, the deputy chief of mission and other embassy representatives attended an annual Kristallnacht (Crystal Night) commemoration ceremony at the Santiago Hebrew School. The deputy chief of mission attended a Kuwaiti government-sponsored event that promoted Islam's peaceful and charitable aspects.

On December 14, the ambassador attended a Hanukkah celebration at La Moneda Palace co-hosted by the minister secretary general of the presidency and the president of the CJCH.

In: Chile
Editor: Garrett M. Ulrich
ISBN: 978-1-61122-031-5


*Chapter 5*

# 2013 INVESTMENT CLIMATE STATEMENT: CHILE*

***Bureau of Economic and Business Affairs***

## OPENNESS TO, AND RESTRICTIONS UPON, FOREIGN INVESTMENT

For the last three decades, Chile has made foreign direct investment (FDI) an essential part of its national development strategy. Chile's sound, market-oriented policies have created significant opportunities for foreign investors to participate in the country's steady economic growth. Chile's business climate is generally straightforward and transparent. Foreign investors receive treatment similar to Chilean nationals in nearly all sectors. There are generally no special exemptions or incentives for FDI as a matter of policy. A broad political consensus on the advantages of foreign investment means that Chile's policies towards FDI are unlikely to change.

FDI in Chile must enter through either of the following mechanisms: the Foreign Investment Statute Decree Law 600 (DL600) or Chapter XIV of the Central Bank's Compendium of Foreign Exchange Regulations (CFER). The minimum investment under DL600 is USD 5,000,000 in currency and USD 2,500,000 in the case of fixed assets, technology, debt capitalization, and profit

* This is an edited, reformatted and augmented version of the Bureau of Economic and Business Affairs Publication, dated February 2013.

reinvestments. FDI valued below these levels but above USD 10,000 is made through Chapter XIV of the Central Bank's CFER.

Chile's openness and transparency to FDI are embodied in DL600. This law has been the main regulatory norm for FDI in Chile during the last 40 years. Under DL600, a foreign investor signs a contract with the Government of Chile (GOC) establishing the terms of the investment. The general regulations, terms, interest, and other modalities of foreign credit contracts as well as surcharges related to total costs to be paid by the debtor, including commissions, taxes, and expenses must also be authorized by the Central Bank of Chile. DL600 allows for capital increases in a given investment.

Chile's Foreign Investment Committee (FIC), the entity responsible for administering DL600, establishes the terms and conditions of the investment. Applications are typically approved within a matter of days and almost always within a month. The FIC's authority to reject a foreign investment is severely limited by the Chilean Constitution. The FIC's decision can be appealed if an investment is rejected.

Chapter XIV establishes regulations that govern foreign exchange operations related to credits, deposits, investments, and capital contributions originating abroad. Investments made under Chapter XIV do not involve signing a contract with the Chilean state. Instead, the Central Bank grants authorization for a given investment. FDI made under Chapter XIV must be in a foreign currency and does not convey any special rights to the investor, such as access to a guaranteed tax rate. The investor must inform the Chilean Central Bank of the investment through a commercial bank or other authorized financial institution. FDI valued at less than USD 10,000 does not require Central Bank approval.

In 2002, the Chilean Government launched an Investment Platform Initiative aimed at attracting international corporations' Latin American headquarters to Chile. As part of this initiative, an eligible company can make use of a variety of incentives, including tax exemptions for overseas shareholders based on certain criteria and a lack of restrictions on domestic borrowing by a platform company. The Initiative addresses the problem of three-way taxation by exempting platform companies from Chilean tax on overseas earnings and provides foreign investors with additional incentives to invest in Chile. This Initiative is meant to foster regional joint ventures between foreign investors and Chilean partners. To facilitate the entry of foreign capital into Chile, the Initiative also allows companies that are already established in the region to move their centers of operation to Chile without incurring the transaction costs involved in selling and re-buying assets.

Increasing public participation complicated investment projects in certain cases in 2012 and created uncertainty for investors. For example, a project by a Brazilian company to build a coal-fired power plant in northern Chile was withdrawn after failing to obtain required environmental approvals, a direct result of significant challenges from an increasingly sophisticated environmental movement.

There are no restrictions on foreign investment in telecommunications, but investors must acquire a license, and the number of licenses available is limited in some new sectors of the industry. Certain types of investment projects require additional authorization beyond that of the FIC. For example, projects in the copper mining sector require the Chilean Copper Commission's authorization; investments in the fishing sector require the approval of the Under-Secretariat of Fishing; authorization from the Bank and Financial Institutions Regulatory Agency is required to operate in the banking sector; and the Securities and Exchange Commission must authorize projects related to insurance and investment funds. Additional authorizations are required from the Pension Funds and Private Health Insurance regulatory agencies to participate in those sectors. For projects with a potential environmental impact, authorization is required from the Environmental Evaluation Service, a decentralized service related to but independent from the Ministry of Environment. Chile also maintains national security related restrictions on investments in the areas of nuclear energy, defense, maritime transportation, real estate, and mining.

Profit remitted, withdrawn or distributed to foreign investors is subject to a withholding tax. Dividends paid to foreign shareholders are subject to an additional 35 percent tax on distribution, but a credit of 17 percent is given against the additional tax where the amounts at issue were subject to Chile's First Category tax. The company must withhold the additional tax. The same tax procedure applies to remittances of profit made to partners and to profit withdrawn by foreigners.

The United States-Chile Free Trade Agreement (FTA) entered into force on January 1, 2004. The chapter on investment is modeled on the standards found in agreements throughout the world such as U.S. bilateral investment treaties and customary international law. The main objective of the FTA chapter is to provide stability and security to investors. It provides six basic forms of protection:

- Non-discriminatory treatment, based on national treatment and most-favored-nation treatment, for investors from either country;

- Freedom from performance requirements;
- Free transfer of investment funds;
- Expropriation only when consistent with international law;
- A minimum standard of treatment in customary international law; and
- The ability to hire key managerial and technical personnel without regard to nationality.

| Measure | Year | Index/Ranking |
|---|---|---|
| TI Corruption Index | 2012 | 72 / 20 (one spot behind U.S.A.) |
| Heritage Economic Freedom | 2012 | 78.3 / 7<br>(three spots ahead of U.S.A.) |
| World Bank Doing Business | 2012 | 37 |
| MCC Gov't Effectiveness | N/A | N/A |
| MCC Rule of Law | N/A | N/A |
| MCC Control of Corruption | N/A | N/A |
| MCC Fiscal Policy | N/A | N/A |
| MCC Trade Policy | N/A | N/A |
| MCC Regulatory Quality | N/A | N/A |
| MCC Business Start Up | N/A | N/A |
| MCC Land Rights Access | N/A | N/A |
| MCC Natural Resource Mgmt | N/A | N/A |

## Conversion and Transfer Policies

Chile's regulation ensures that capital markets are well developed and open to both foreign portfolio investment and FDI. In May 2000, Chile eliminated the one-year withholding period requirement for foreign capital entering the country under Chapter XIV. This type of investment capital may now be repatriated immediately without penalty.

A second major initiative in 2000 was the discontinuation of the use of the "encaje" or lock-in, which required foreign investors to deposit 30 percent of foreign-sourced loans and portfolio investment with the Central Bank in a non-interest-bearing account for up two years. The Central Bank reserves the right to re-impose the "encaje" mechanism if needed in the future.

About a decade ago the Chilean government delivered important reforms and measures aimed at promoting savings in investment securities, including by exempting capital gains taxes on highly traded stocks of publicly traded companies, lowering taxes for foreign investors on interest payments, and advancing in the integration of Chilean capital markets to the international financing market.

A second set of reforms in 2005-06 aimed at promoting broader financing alternatives of high growth, emerging companies (small- to medium-sized enterprises, SMEs) and tax incentives for the development of a local risk capital fund management industry. In June 2007, the GOC passed Law 20.190 that introduced tax incentives to promote venture capital. The law improves the availability of financial resources for SMEs and provides tax benefits to public as well as private venture capital funds. Law 20.190 authorizes Chile's Development Promotion Agency (CORFO, www.corfo.cl) to take an equity position of up to 40 percent in specialized venture capital funds. It also allows banks to invest up to the equivalent of one percent of their asset base in venture capital through investment fund administrators and subsidiaries.

A third capital market reform was introduced in 2010, aimed at increasing security levels of financial transactions, stronger custodial, clearing and payment, and reinforcing regulatory and supervision capabilities. These improvements involved guidance in the form of regulations and the sharing of best practices related to investment funds, derivatives and insurance companies. This set of reforms aims to improve current levels of competition in the credit market by increasing available credit instruments and to improve consumer information. The reform also increases liquidity, deepens credit markets, improves flexibility for investment funds, creates Exchange Traded Funds (ETFs), allows access to secondary markets, and fosters investment in mutual and investment funds. Another initiative already underway, the Bicentennial Capital Market Reform, aims to modernize and deepen the Chilean capital market; provide financial protection to consumers; and improve insurance and banking regulations.

Investors, importers, and others are guaranteed access to foreign exchange in the official inter-bank currency market without restriction.

The Central Bank reserves the right to deny access to the inter-bank currency market for royalty payments in excess of five percent of sales. The same restriction applies to payments for the use of patents that exceed five percent of sales. In such cases, firms would have access to the informal market. The Chilean tax service reserves the right to prevent royalties of over five percent of sales from being counted as expenses for domestic tax purposes.

Under the Investment Chapter of the U.S.–Chile FTA, each government must allow transfers of covered investment to be made freely and without delay into and out of its territory. These include transfers of profits, royalties, sales proceeds, and other remittances related to the investment. However, for certain types of short-term capital flows, the chapter allows Chile to impose transfer restrictions for 12 months as long as those restrictions do not substantially impede transfers. If restrictions are found to impede transfers substantially, damages accrue from the date of the initiation of the measure.

## Expropriation and Compensation

Chilean law grants the government authority to expropriate property, including property of foreign investors, only for public or national interests, on a non-discriminatory basis and in accordance with due process of law.

The law requires the payment of compensation without delay at fair market value, in addition to any applicable interest. The government has not nationalized a private firm since 1973.

## Dispute Settlement

Disputes involving U.S. investors have been typically settled in negotiations between the investor and the appropriate government entity. Disputes have been referred to the local judicial system although the time required for resolution may make this an unattractive option for foreign investors. Because of high case loads, understaffing and antiquated procedures, resolution of business disputes in the civil court system often takes four to five years. Accordingly, litigants often choose to settle out of court. A suit may also be brought in court under expedited procedures involving the abrogation of constitutional rights.

The FTA Investment Chapter provides a mechanism for investors to pursue a claim against a host government that is in breach of the FTA's investment obligations, an investment agreement, or an investment authorization. An exception is disputes related to investment authorizations under DL600, which are *not* subject to this mechanism. Only agreements signed within two years of the FTA's entry into force may make use of this mechanism. Under this section, the investor pursuing a claim may submit a claim under the International Center for Settlement of Investment Disputes (ICSID) Convention or under the United Nations Commission on International Trade Law (UNCITRAL) arbitration rules. Any other mutually agreed upon

arbitral institution may also be utilized. Rules agreed upon by the parties will govern the proceedings except to the extent that they are inconsistent with the FTA. An investor must give notice of intent to arbitrate at least 90 days before submitting a claim, and must wait at least six months from the time of the event which gave rise to the claim before initiating a proceeding. All claims must be brought within three years of the date when the claimant acquired knowledge of the breach and/or injury.

The FTA chapter on investments encourages consultations or negotiations before recourse to dispute settlement mechanisms. If the parties fail to resolve the matter, a claim for arbitration can be submitted by the investor. Provisions in Section C of the FTA ensure that the proceedings are transparent by requiring that all documents submitted to or issued by the tribunal be available to the public, and by stipulating that proceedings be public. The tribunal must also accept amicus curiae submissions. The FTA chapter on investments establishes clear and specific terms for making proceedings more efficient and avoiding frivolous claims. Domestic law is to be applied to all contracts. However, arbitral tribunals decide disputes in accordance with FTA obligations and applicable international law.

The judicial system in Chile is generally transparent and independent. The likelihood of government intervention in court cases is low. If a state-dependent firm is involved in the dispute, the GOC may become directly involved through the State Defense Council. In cases where courts determine a firm is bankrupt, a receiver is named to distribute the debtor's remaining assets to the creditors.

## PERFORMANCE REQUIREMENTS/INCENTIVES

Chile's Foreign Investment Committee does not apply performance requirements in its review of projects. The investment chapter in the U.S.–Chile FTA establishes rules prohibiting performance requirements that apply to all investments, whether by a third party or domestic investors.

The FTA investment chapter also regulates the use of mandatory performance requirements as a condition for receiving incentives and spells out the exceptions. These include government procurement, qualifications for export and foreign aid programs, and non-discriminatory health, safety, and environmental requirements.

Chile does not subsidize foreign investment nor does it offer any special tax exemptions. There are, however, some regional incentives linked to

isolated geographical zones and to the information technology sector. These benefits relate to co-financing of feasibility studies as well as to incentives for the purchase of land in industrial zones, the hiring of local labor, and the facilitation of project financing. Other important incentives include accelerated depreciation accounting for tax purposes, special tax treatment for retained earnings, and legal guarantees for remitting profits and capital.

Chile has other special incentive programs aimed mostly at promoting investment and employment in remote or disadvantaged regions, the development of new businesses, support for micro-, small-, and medium-sized enterprises, and promotion of technological innovation.

Since 2001, CORFO has implemented the "Chile Invests" plan with the goal of fostering FDI outside the Santiago Metropolitan Region in certain sectors. A key objective of the plan is to encourage investment in areas of non-traditional technology such as biotechnology, research and development of new materials, electronics and engineering processes, and new production techniques to increase the value added to natural resource exports. The plan also promotes investment in the energy sector mainly for non-conventional renewable energy projects. CORFO provides co-financing programs to pre-investment feasibility studies for projects using renewable non-conventional energy resources.

The Arica Law of 2001 grants tax credits to companies in the provinces of Arica and Parinacota. Investment projects amounting to over 2,000 UTM (about USD 145,000) in Arica are eligible for a tax credit of 30 percent of the value of the fixed physical assets (40 percent for tourism projects). Investment projects totaling more than 1,000 UTM (about USD 76,000) in Parinacota are eligible for a tax credit of 40 percent of the value of the fixed physical assets. These incentives are available until December 31, 2030. [NOTE: The Unidad Tributaria Mensual (UTM) is an inflation-indexed measure of value, adjusted on a monthly basis. On January 18, 2013, 1 UTM was equivalent to about USD 85.

A third investment promotion plan for the province of Tierra del Fuego in Region XII (Magallanes) is available for mining, manufacturing, transport, fishing and tourism companies that produce goods or services made up of at least 25 percent of local labor and inputs.

Other investment incentives have been introduced through the "Chile Competes Plan." The Plan includes an exemption from the income tax normally paid by institutional investors, such as mutual funds and pension funds, on earnings from the transfer of corporate stock that is publicly traded, or bonds or other publicly offered securities representing debt issued by the

Central Bank of Chile, the Chilean Government, or by companies incorporated in Chile.

In January 2011, the Ministry of Economy, using CORFO, established a three-year, USD 40 million program, known as "StartUp Chile," whereby selected entrepreneurs receives a USD 40,000 grant and a Chilean work visa to develop a "start up" business in Chile. Upon admittance into the program, an entrepreneur is given six months to develop a project and then promote it through a series of pitches and seminars at local universities, corporate meetings and other community outreach.

## RIGHT TO PRIVATE OWNERSHIP AND ESTABLISHMENT

Except for the limitations in the fisheries and media sectors noted above, Chile does not, in general, restrict the right to private ownership or establishment. Section 24 of Article 19 of the Constitution establishes the "absolute, exclusive, inalienable and permanent domain" of the Chilean state over all mineral, hydrocarbon, and fossil fuel deposits within Chilean territory. Under Chilean law, the Government may grant concession rights to individuals and companies for exploration and development of these natural resources for a finite period. There are also national security-related measures regarding the purchase of real estate by foreigners in certain geographic areas, such as near land borders with Chile's neighbors.

## PROTECTION OF PROPERTY RIGHTS

Because of concerns about its commitment to the protection of intellectual property rights (IPR), Chile has been on the Special 301 Priority Watch List (PWL) since January 8, 2007. The Chilean government has undertaken a number of legislative reforms to strengthen its IPR regime and bring it in line with international commitments, including the U.S.-Chile Free Trade Agreement (FTA). However, there are still substantive deficiencies in Chile's IPR laws and enforcement of existing IPR protections. Of particular concern are inadequate patent and test data protection in the pharmaceutical sector; copyright piracy of movies, music, and software; and Chile's failure to protect encrypted program-carrying satellite signals.

The 2012 Special 301 Report notes steps Chile has taken to address outstanding IPR issues under the United States-Chile Free Trade Agreement, including accession to the Convention Relating to the Distribution of Programme Carrying Signals Transmitted by Satellite and the Trademark Law Treaty. Chile has also taken, the report notes, steps toward acceding to and ratifying the International Convention for the Protection of New Varieties of Plants (UPOV). The report urges Chile to: implement an effective system for addressing patent issues expeditiously in connection with applications to market pharmaceutical products; implement protections against the circumvention of technological protection measures and protections for encrypted program-carrying satellite signals; ensure that effective administrative and judicial procedures and deterrent remedies are made available to IPR holders; provide adequate protections concerning undisclosed test or other data generated to obtain marketing approval for pharmaceutical products; and amend its internet service provider liability regime to permit effective action against piracy over the internet.

The U.S.-Chile FTA seeks to strengthen protection for valid patents and their accompanying clinical test data. For example, the FTA provides for the extension of the protection period for patents when there are unjustified delays in the patenting process. The FTA also requires parties to protect confidential information provided to authorities in order to obtain marketing or health permits for pharmaceutical products and agricultural chemicals. In addition, the FTA establishes the obligation to undertake reasonable efforts to extend patent rights to qualifying plants.

In 2012, the United States and Chile held several meetings to exchange information and review implementation of the IPR provisions of the FTA. In addition to urging Chile to address IPR issues in the pharmaceutical industry, the United States has asked Chile to implement protections against the circumvention of technological protection measures, to implement protections for encrypted program-carrying satellite signals, and to ensure that effective administrative and judicial procedures and deterrent remedies are made available to rights holders.

Chile has been a member of the World Intellectual Property Organization (WIPO) since 1975 and joined the Treaties on Copyright and Performances and Phonograms in April 2001. Chile approved legislation to comply with TRIPS obligations related to industrial property in December 2004. The law provides, among other protections, for expedited court proceedings and the authority to seize illegal copies of patented products. In 2008, Chile ratified the Patent Cooperation Treaty (PCT), which came into force in June 2009.

The U.S. and Chile have committed to making a system available for the resolution of disputes regarding internet domain names. This follows international standards with respect to problems such as the cyber piracy of brands and trademarks for country domain names. Furthermore, both countries committed to creating a database containing information on individuals who have registered higher-level domain names. This database will protect the personal data of those who have registered.

## TRANSPARENCY OF THE REGULATORY SYSTEM

Chilean regulatory systems tend to be transparent, and government regulators generally have little discretion in carrying out their duties. While rulemaking processes do not generally include formal provisions for public hearing or comment, opening a business is normally easier in Chile than in many other developing countries. The World Bank's "Doing Business 2013" report ranks Chile 32$^{nd}$ of 185 economies (previously 27$^{th}$ of 183 in 2011) for ease of starting a business. The U.S.–Chile FTA establishes some additional obligations for transparency in regulatory processes.

## EFFICIENT CAPITAL MARKETS AND PORTFOLIO INVESTMENT

Chile's capital markets are well-developed and open to foreign portfolio investors. Credit is allocated on market terms and is available to foreigners although the Central Bank does reserve the right to restrict foreign investors' access to internal credit if a credit shortage exists. To date, this authority has not been exercised.

Publicly traded Chilean companies attract substantial international investment. In late 2000, the Chilean Congress approved legislation on public stock tenders that provides greater legal protection of minority shareholder rights.

In November 2001, the core measures in the far-reaching "Capital Market Reform I" came into force. This first reform: provided more flexibility for the insurance and mutual-fund industries; abolished income tax on capital gains from the sale of frequently traded shares; promoted voluntary (pre-tax) contributions by employees to pension plans (mirroring the U.S. 401K option);

created five funds with different risk-return profiles instead of a single option administered by the private pension fund administrators (AFPs); and created asset-management entities to manage several types of funds, such as mutual funds, investment funds and mortgage companies.

Capital market reform leveled the playing field for foreign investors in the local market and those who invest in Chilean bonds abroad. This has slowly increased demand for local debt instruments among new foreign investors.

In June 2007, "Capital Market Reform II" entered into force to promote the development of the venture capital industry, strengthen the stock and exchange markets, deepen other Chilean financial markets, broaden the existing scheme of voluntary contributions for pensions, improve standards for corporate governance in accordance with OECD standards, and increase supervision over the market. In September 2009, the GOC introduced "Capital Market Reform III" aimed at providing better levels and quality of credit to SMEs and internationalizing the Chilean capital market. Passed in 2010, this third reform increased liquidity and depth of the capital market, enlarged the financial markets, promoted competition within the credit market, and facilitated integration of Chilean capital markets by promoting participation of non-residents. One particular reform, Law 20,448, provided grounds for the growth of Exchange Traded Funds (EFTs) in Chile by amending the mutual fund statute in order to allow the payment of shares by contributing a basket of securities that mirrors the investment portfolio of the fund.

In 2010, President Sebastian Pinera's government introduced a new package of capital reforms called the "Bicentennial Capital Market Reform." This new reform consists of over 20 separate bills aiming to: deepen integration with international capital markets; introduce regulatory measures to promote innovation and undertakings; improve competition, oversight and transparency; increase liquidity and access to financial markets; and improve standards for corporate governance and customer protection.

Under the U.S.-Chile FTA, U.S. insurance firms have full rights to establish subsidiaries or joint ventures for all insurance sectors, with limited exceptions. A program is underway to phase in insurance branching rights and to modify Chile's legislation to open cross-border supply of key insurance sectors such as marine, aviation, and transport (MAT) insurance, and insurance brokerage of reinsurance. U.S. banks and securities firms are allowed to establish branches and subsidiaries and may invest in local firms without restriction, except under very limited circumstances. U.S. financial institutions are also able to offer financial services to citizens participating in Chile's privatized voluntary saving plans, and they have gained increased market access to Chile's mandatory social security system. U.S.-based firms are allowed to offer services in Chile in areas such as financial information, data processing, and financial advisory services, with limited exceptions. Under the measures outlined in "Capital Market Reform III," Chilean mutual funds are permitted to use foreign-based portfolio managers.

In May 2011, the stock markets of Chile, Peru and Colombia merged to become the second largest trading market in Latin America after Brazil. This market alliance, known as the Integrated Latin American Market (MILA) hopes to better expose investors to assets linked to the region's natural resources. Chile's IPSA Index is a total return index and is composed of 40 highly traded stocks. The IPSA has been calculated since 1977 and is revised on a quarterly basis.

The main institutional investors and suppliers of capital to local companies are the pension fund administrators (AFP) as well as insurance companies, mutual funds and banks. More than half of the instruments issued in the fixed-income market are held by institutional investors.

Pension funds are the largest institutional investors followed by insurance companies. As of September 2012, Chile's seven AFPs managed a total investment portfolio of USD 151.6 billion, representing about 76 percent of Chile's GDP. The pension funds administered by the AFPs belong to 9.2 million contributors. As of September 2012, the total resources under AFP administration were distributed in five different types of funds of varying degrees of risk. As of July 2012, accumulated savings in the voluntary contributions system (APV) of the AFP system totaled USD 4.3 billion that belong to 735,170 contributors.

The GOC has been raising the percentage of pension funds that can be invested overseas. In 2008, a reform package of the pension system was approved by Congress increasing the threshold for pension fund administrators to invest abroad (from 30 to 60 percent of their funds). The reform package also set the foundation on which to build a "solidarity pillar" to increase coverage among lower-income contributors and self-employed workers and expand social security assistance coverage. Total spending in 2012 on "solidarity pension payments" reached USD 286.2 million.

As of September 2012, insurance companies managed more than USD 6 billion in assets. Insurance companies invest a major share of their portfolio in fixed-income securities.

The Chilean banking system is sound, competitive, and meets Basel standards. There are currently 25 banks operating in Chile, and 12 are foreign-owned representational branches. Only one bank is completely owned by

Chilean economic interests (BCI). The rest have some level of incorporation with foreign institutions. Foreign banks can compete on the same terms as their domestic rivals. There are also five local savings and loan corporations, and one state-owned bank, Banco Estado, which is the nation's third largest. Private banks manage most corporate business.

The Chilean banking industry is subject to strict limits on lending to a single debtor or group of related companies. This is capped at five percent of the capital and reserves of a bank for collateral-free loans and at 25 percent for collateralized loans (fixed assets).

In 2009, Chile enacted several reforms as part of the process to join the Organization for Economic Cooperation and Development (OECD). One of these reforms was a law that Chile enacted in 2009 allowing for the exchange of tax information between tax authorities, including information based on bank account activity (information previously restricted under Chilean law). As of September 2012, there was a low level of systemic risk within the system due to a sound regulatory framework. As a result, the rate of non-performing loans remained low, at 2.75 percent, and the aggregate loans-to-deposits ratio was stable at 119 percent.

**Summary of Chilean Banking System (November 2012)**

| | |
|---|---|
| Total Loans | USD 220.1 billion |
| Deposits | USD 182.7 billion |
| Total Assets | USD 294.4 billion |

Source: Chile's Superintendence of Banks and Financial Institutions.

General Information on the Financial Market (November 2012)

- Banks and Financial Institutions: 25 participants. Total Loans: USD 220.1 billion
- Pension Funds: 6 administrators. Funds under management: USD 151.6 billion
- Insurance Companies: 59 (26 general insurers, 33 life insurers).

According to the World Economic Forum's Global Competitiveness Report for 2012-2013, Chile is the most competitive country of South America and the third most competitive of the Americas after the U.S. and Canada. Chile is ranked 33rd in the world.

# Competition from State-Owned Enterprises (SOEs)

Chile has relatively few state-owned enterprises (SOEs), most having been privatized during the military government's economic reforms between 1974 and 1989. Notable SOE's are the national copper company, CODELCO; the national petroleum company, ENAP; the National Postal System (Correos de Chile); and the state-owned bank, Banco Estado.

In general, private enterprise is allowed to compete with public enterprise under the same terms and conditions (e.g., there are many private copper mines and private banks). However, there are specific areas where this does not hold and SOEs enjoy special advantages. For example, ENAP is the only refining company in Chile.

Most SOEs in Chile are structured so that the company management reports to a board of directors, which includes the relevant government minister (e.g., the Minister of Mining sits on ENAP's board of directors). Most board members are independent representatives from the private sector and academia, or from that industry's main labor union or trade association. Board members are usually designated by the President of Chile.

Chile passed a law in October 2009 which modifies CODELCO's corporate governing structure. The law removes the Ministers of Finance and Mining and a representative of the military from the board of directors. It also expands the board to nine members, three of whom are designated by the President of Chile, two of whom are nominated by CODELCO's labor unions and approved by the President of Chile, and four of whom are elected by the Consejo de Alta Dirección Pública (Chile's independent committee that makes high-level civil service appointments) and subsequently approved by the President of Chile.

Chile has two sovereign wealth funds constituted principally from state copper revenues. The Economic and Social Stabilization Fund (FEES) was established in 2007 and was valued at USD 14.9 billion in November 2012. The Reserve Pension Fund was established in 2006 and was valued at USD 5.8 billion in November 2012. The stated purpose of this fund is to assist the Government with payments to those eligible to receive pensions but who remain indigent (Chile uses a privatized pension system). A third sovereign wealth fund, called the Bicentennial Fund, encourages Chileans to study abroad through the use of government funded scholarships.

The sovereign wealth funds are administered by the Chilean Central Bank, at the direction of the Ministry of Finance. The Ministry of Finance receives advice on policy related to the funds from an external Finance Committee made up of independent advisors. The Ministry of Finance publishes monthly, quarterly, and yearly reports on the funds.

## Corporate Social Responsibility (CSR)

There is general awareness of corporate social responsibility among both producers and consumers in Chile. As part of the OECD accession process, Chile passed a law in September 2009 setting out new rules to help bolster corporate social responsibility.

## Political Violence

The incidence of terrorist activity and civil disturbance is generally low in Chile, and the violence that has occurred has had little impact on the Chilean economy. Crime rates are moderate throughout the country, and the vast majority of crimes are nonviolent. During the last 10 years there have been relatively few incidents of politically motivated attacks on investment projects or installations. In 2012, there were occasional incidents of vandalism of storefronts and public transport during student protests over education reform, some of which included violent incidents. Incidents of anti-American sentiment and civil disorder are rare, and there have been no attacks known to be attributable to international terrorist organizations. However, since 2007 Chile has experienced a number of small-scale bombings targeting mostly banks, but also a police station, a political memorial and the U.K. Embassy, the offices of a major newspaper and magazine publisher, and a prominent Catholic cathedral. Anarchist groups have claimed credit for some of the bombings. There have also been violent incidents on farms and forestry plantations in south-central Chile, resulting in three deaths in 2012. Many of these incidents are related to the land claims and other grievances of indigenous people (the Mapuche Native American group) in regions VIII (Bio-Bio) and IX (Araucania).

## CORRUPTION

Corruption in Chile is generally limited. Since 2003, Chile has had laws in place that establish a more efficient and professional civil service through performance-based incentives and a reduction in political appointee positions in public service positions. In 2005, the GOC passed a law to regulate political party and candidate financing to further deter corrupt government practices.

Chile has signed and ratified the Organization of American States (OAS) Convention against Corruption. Chile is also a signatory to the OECD Convention on Combating Bribery, fulfilling the necessary accession processes, including implementation of its Anti-Bribery Convention obligations.

In 2007, a new law came into force that provides protection for public employees who denounce irregularities or violations in accountability standards and at the same time, Chile ratified the United Nations Convention against Corruption. In 2009, Chile passed a transparency law obligating government offices to public information about expenditures, employee salaries, and other fiscal data. It also mandates that citizens be provided up-to-date information on how to access government services and request information. The law created an autonomous Transparency Council which is charged with implementing the requirements of the law. The Pinera administration has launched a campaign to educate citizens about their right to access public information and created Chile Atiende, an online and in-person platform to streamline access to common government services.

Chile is an active member of the Open Government Partnership (OGP).

## BILATERAL INVESTMENT AGREEMENTS

In 1991, Chile became a signatory of the Washington Convention of 1965, which created the International Center for Settlement of Investment Disputes (ICSID). Since then, Chile has negotiated numerous Bilateral Investment Treaties (BITs) through which Chile provides additional protection to foreign investment flows. According to information provided by the Government of Chile to ICSID, as of the end of 2012, Chile had signed 53 BITs, of which 39 are in force. There are agreements in force with Argentina, Australia, Austria, Belgium, Bolivia, China, Costa Rica, Croatia, Cuba, Czech Republic, Denmark, Dominican Republic, Ecuador, El Salvador, Finland, France,

Germany, Greece, Guatemala, Honduras, Italy, Malaysia, Nicaragua, Norway, Panama, Paraguay, Peru, Philippines, Poland, Portugal, Romania, Spain, Sweden, Switzerland, Ukraine, the United Kingdom, Uruguay, and Venezuela. Those BITs signed but not in force include Brazil, Colombia, Egypt, Hungary, Iceland, Indonesia, Lebanon, Netherlands, New Zealand, South Africa, Tunisia, Turkey and Vietnam.

Chile has a number of double taxation treaties in force: Australia, Belgium, Brazil, Canada, Colombia, Croatia, Denmark, Ecuador, France, Ireland, Malaysia, Mexico, New Zealand, Norway, Paraguay, Peru, Poland, Portugal, Russia, South Korea, Spain, Sweden, Switzerland and the United Kingdom.

Chile and the United States have signed the U.S.-Chile Treaty to Avoid Double Taxation, which addresses certain tax-related obligations for U.S. companies operating in Chile. In May 2012 President Obama submitted the treaty to the U.S. Senate for ratification. As of January 2013, the Government of Chile has not submitted the treaty to the Chilean Congress for ratification.

## OPIC and Other Investment Insurance Programs

A Bilateral Investment Agreement with the Overseas Private Investment Corporation (OPIC) took effect in 1984. Chile is a party to the convention of the World Bank's Multilateral Investment Guarantee Agency (MIGA).

## Labor

Chile has enjoyed generally calm labor relations over the last decade, but strikes do occur. Strikes and public protests have been concentrated in the mining, health, education, transportation, and civil service sectors.

Union membership is voluntary, and approximately 11 percent of the non-public workforce and 13.8 percent of the total workforce is unionized. Multiple unions exist in many companies, and management can negotiate collective agreements with any of the unions or with ad hoc groups of workers. Unions can form confederations or nationwide labor centrals and can affiliate with international labor federations. Contracts are normally negotiated at the company level. Multi-company bargaining is permitted on a voluntary basis. Minimum wage, working hours, overtime, paid annual vacations, and holidays are all established by law. Women are entitled to state-funded maternity leave for a period of six weeks before and six months after childbirth. Layoffs are not permitted between conception and one year after the female employee has returned from maternity leave.

Top executive salaries are on a par with European countries, although well below those in the U.S. Chile allows companies to deduct set training costs (up to one percent of annual payroll) from corporate tax payments. A company can also use 10 percent of the rebate to finance an analysis of its training needs, and 15 percent to run a training department.

On January 1, 2005, the maximum number of labor hours per week was reduced from 48 to 45 without any loss of salary to the employees. This is now the standard work week in Chile.

Subject to certain exceptions, Chilean nationals must comprise no less than 85 percent of the workforce of companies employing more than 25 persons.

A 2007 subcontracting law defines outsourcing as two different activities: subcontracting and the supply of outside labor. Subcontracting is when a company permanently outsources a specific process to another firm which takes full responsibility for it, carrying it out with its own employees. However, the law does not permit companies to outsource its main economic activity. Regarding outside workers, the law limits this to "temporary" labor, defined as those employed for periods of up to 90 (or in some cases 180) days during an "emergency." Additionally, only firms that register as suppliers of temporary labor and set up guarantees against their obligations to their own workers are allowed to fulfill this function. The law also sets limits on the number of staff that can be used on short-term jobs.

## FOREIGN TRADE ZONES/FREE PORTS

Chile has two tax-free zones: one in the northern port of Iquique (Region I) and the other in the southern city of Punta Arenas (Region XII). Merchants and manufacturers in these zones are exempt from corporate tax, VAT, and customs duties. Businesses can re-export goods without paying taxes but must pay VAT (19 percent) and import duties when goods leave the zone to be used/sold in other regions of Chile. The same exemptions also apply to manufacturers in the Chacalluta and Las Americas Industrial Park in Arica (in the XV Arica and Parinacota Region created in October 2007). Mining, fishing and financial services are not eligible for free zone concessions. Management companies and firms established in the free zone are exempt from payment of tariffs, VAT, other charges on imports, first category income tax under the Income Tax Law, and payment of VAT on goods and services for all their operations in the free zone.

## FOREIGN DIRECT INVESTMENT STATISTICS

Today more than 3,000 companies from 60 countries have operations in Chile. Over the last decade, FDI has represented an annual average of around 6.5 percent of Chile's GDP. The United Nations Conference on Trade and Development (UNCTAD) World Investment Report for 2011 placed Chile sixth in the world and first in Latin America in its FDI Attraction Index, which measures countries' success in attracting FDI over a rolling three-year period.

Between 1974 and 2011, the mining sector attracted 34.1 percent of implemented FDI under DL600, followed by services (22.4 percent); electricity, gas and water (18.4 percent); manufacturing (10.9 percent); transportation and communications (11.1 percent); and construction (1.7 percent).

Although figures for the total 2012 authorized and implemented FDI are not available yet, through October of 2012 authorized FDI stood at USD 16.1 billion, up 21.6 percent on authorized FDI for all of 2011 (USD 13.7 billion). During this timeframe, the mining sector accounted for 56.7 percent of authorized FDI (USD 9.4 billion), followed by the service sector (18.5 percent); transport and communications (10.0 percent); electricity, gas and water (9.6 percent); and manufacturing (4.8 percent).

According to the Central Bank, implemented (as compared to authorized) FDI in Chile reached a record of USD 12.3 billion in the first three months of 2012, representing an 80.2 percent increase over inflows from the same period in 2011. The mining sector was at the forefront of the historic wave of capital, accounting for 60.3 percent of implemented FDI at USD 1.1 billion, followed by the gas, electricity and water sector, at 14.2 percent of total implemented FDI (USD 250.8 million). The manufacturing sector accounted for 12.7 percent (USD 224.9 million) and transportation and communication represented 7.4 percent (USD 130.6 million) of all implemented FDI.

According to the Central Bank, in 2011 implemented FDI was a record USD 17.5 billion, representing a 16.1 percent increase over 2010 FDI (USD 15.1 billion). Actual implemented or realized FDI in 2011 through the D.L.

600 totaled USD 4.1 billion, while FDI realized from the U.S. from January through September 2012 amounted to USD 3.9 million.

In 2011, Canada was the largest investor in Chile with 59 percent of total implemented FDI in the country, with projects totaling USD 8.2 billion. Canada was followed by Japan (12 percent), Spain (7 percent), the United States (6 percent) and Australia (4 percent).

**FDI (DL600) by Sector (USD million, nominal)**

| Sector | 1974-2008 | 2008 | 2009 | 2010* | 2011* |
|---|---|---|---|---|---|
| Agriculture | 268,918 | 940 | 0 | 2,000 | 47,504 |
| Forestry | 455,984 | 80,386 | 29,081 | 12,061 | 7,889 |
| Fishing/aquiculture | 319,226 | 10,998 | 0 | 0 | 0 |
| Mining | 23,538,324 | 2,366,188 | 1,010,926 | 732,078 | 2,489,023 |
| Food, beverages and Tobacco | 2,347,441 | 49,850 | 55,186 | 4,000 | 49,846 |
| Wood and paper | 1,201,922 | 53,851 | 1,474 | 6,560 | 570 |
| Chemicals | 2,929,661 | 1,469 | 33,142 | 0 | 9,999 |
| Other manufacturing | 1,622,855 | 112,165 | 367,950 | 73,413 | 157,938 |
| Electricity, gas, water | 14,363,530 | 1,409,913 | 305,976 | 87,806 | 209,953 |
| Construction | 1,426,955 | 2,121 | 0 | 7,308 | 0 |
| Wholesale, retail trade | 1,586,591 | 2,702 | 2,702 | 2,702 | 56,660 |
| Transport, storage | 1,159,345 | 425,985 | 8,028 | 276,294 | 125,670 |
| Communication | 6,891,408 | 283,225 | 194,547 | 63,051 | 94,122 |
| Financial services (1) | 6,937,828 | 207,571 | 317,374 | 43,058 | 56,045 |
| Insurance | 2,130,174 | 26,158 | 400 | 20,627 | 722,243 |
| Engineering – business Services | 847,857 | 113,628 | 60,486 | 34,005 | 108,695 |
| Sewage, sanitation and similar services | 522,644 | 0 | 0 | 0 | 0 |
| Other Services (2) | 1,349,813 | 14,461 | 16,606 | 6,505 | 3,817 |
| Total | 69,900,476 | 5,162,229 | 5,082,000 | 1,778,419 | 4,140,074 |

Source: Foreign Investment Committee. (* provisional figures as of December 31, 2012)

(1) Includes banking, investment companies, investment and risk capital funds and other financial services; (2) Includes restaurants and hotels, real estate activities, social and related community services, recreation.

**United States FDI to Chile Under DL600: 1974-2011**
**(USD thousand, nominal)**

| Period | U.S.A. Total Value |
|---|---|
| 1974-90 | 2,462,409 |
| 1991 | 350,245 |
| 1992 | 299,888 |
| 1993 | 606,159 |
| 1994 | 995,783 |
| 1995 | 1,498,332 |
| 1996 | 2,279,315 |
| 1997 | 887,366 |
| 1998 | 1,343,719 |
| 1999 | 1,388,730 |
| 2000 | 788,563 |
| 2001 | 1,808,061 |
| 2002 | 550,951 |
| 2003 | 373.374 |
| 2004 | 124,537 |
| 2005 | 9,242 |
| 2006 | 337,573 |
| 2007 | 337,573 |
| 2008 | 551,923 |
| 2009 | 2,860,451 |
| 2010* | 292,420 |
| 2011* | 210,930 |
| TOTAL | 20,156,947 |

Source: Foreign Investment Committee; (*provisional figures as of December 31, 2011.

The U.S. was the single largest direct investor in Chile from 1984-2011, accounting for 26.4 percent of implemented FDI from 1974 – 2010, totaling over USD 20 billion. U.S. FDI to Chile in 2011 was USD 34.2 billion, down 5.5 percent from 2010. The service sector represented about 33 percent of U.S. FDI in Chile in 2011, followed by the mining sector (27.6 percent); electricity, gas and water (14 percent); manufacturing (12.5 percent); and transportation and communications (10.5 percent). Canada, Japan, Spain, and Mexico –have also been significant investors in Chile in recent years.

According to Central Bank statistics, between 1990 and June 2011 Chilean investment abroad totaled USD 62.7 billion distributed over 70 countries. During that period, ten countries accounted for 92 percent of Chilean FDI abroad: Argentina (32 percent of total out-bound FDI), Brazil (18 percent), Peru (17 percent), Colombia (13 percent), and the United States (7 percent, totaling USD 3.7 billion). Mexico, Panama, Australia, Uruguay and Belgium round out the top ten destination countries for Chilean FDI during the period.

In 2011, over 1,000 Chilean companies combined to invest USD 5.8 billion abroad. In 2011, Peru was the largest recipient of Chilean FDI abroad at USD 1.2 billion, followed by Uruguay and Colombia at USD 950 million and USD 937 million, respectively.

# INDEX

## A

abuse, viii, 41, 42, 43, 45, 46, 54, 55, 57, 60, 61, 63
access, 2, 3, 6, 12, 14, 16, 44, 45, 47, 48, 49, 52, 53, 55, 56, 59, 63, 73, 78, 81, 87, 88, 89, 93
accessibility, 59
accommodations, 44
accountability, 93
accounting, 17, 34, 84, 96, 98
accreditation, 73
adjustment, 31
administrators, 67, 73, 81, 88, 89, 90
adolescents, 58, 67
age, 31, 32, 37, 38, 54, 57, 58, 66, 67, 72
agencies, 39, 52, 53, 59, 66, 73
aggression, 62
agricultural sector, 64, 69
agriculture, 65, 66, 67
anti-Semitism, ix, 41, 71, 74, 75
appointments, 52, 91
appropriations, 15
Appropriations Act, 24
arbitration, 64, 82, 83
Argentina, 38, 39, 40, 93, 98
armed forces, 42, 52, 73, 74
arrest, 46, 47, 61, 62, 63
arson, 60
Asia, 3, 17
assets, viii, 27, 29, 30, 31, 32, 33, 52, 65, 77, 78, 83, 84, 89, 90
asylum, 50
audits, 52
Austria, 93
authority(s), 18, 39, 42, 44, 46, 47, 49, 51, 54, 55, 57, 61, 78, 82, 86, 87, 90
autonomy, 11, 17
average earnings, 30, 31, 38
awareness, 55, 63, 66, 92

## B

bail, 42, 43, 47
banking, 4, 79, 81, 89, 90, 97
banking industry, 90
banking sector, 79
banks, 32, 39, 81, 88, 89, 92
bargaining, 64, 65, 94
barriers, 18, 20, 36, 51, 63
barriers to entry, 36
base, 32, 81
Belgium, 93, 94, 99
beneficiaries, 28, 31, 34
benefits, 8, 28, 30, 32, 33, 34, 35, 36, 37, 38, 59, 62, 64, 81, 84
beverages, 97
*Bilateral*, vii, 1, 18, 93, 94
biomass, 20
biotechnology, 84

births, 3
board members, 91
Bolivia, 67, 93
bonds, 34, 39, 84, 88
bonuses, 36
branching, 88
Brazil, 22, 89, 94, 98
broadcast media, 49
businesses, 56, 64, 68, 84

## C

campaigns, 55
candidates, 9, 10
capital flows, 82
capital gains, 80, 87
capital markets, 80, 81, 87, 88
carbon, 20
caregiving, 35, 37
Caribbean, 23
cash, 8
censorship, 45
center-left coalition, 21
certification, 67
challenges, 2, 6, 14, 28, 38, 79
chat rooms, 49
chemicals, 86
child labor, viii, 41, 66, 67
child pornography, 58
children, viii, 14, 32, 41, 53, 55, 57, 58, 59, 60, 63, 65, 66, 67, 73
Chilean model, vii, 27
China, 12, 93
cities, 74
citizens, 15, 29, 46, 51, 52, 60, 63, 88, 93
civil disorder, 92
civil service, 91, 93, 94
civil society, 4, 52, 58, 66
classes, 74
clean energy, vii, 1, 15, 20
climate, vii, ix, 77
coal, 20, 79
coercion, 43, 56
collaboration, 18, 20
collateral, 90
collective bargaining, 64, 65
Colombia, 19, 25, 89, 94, 99
commerce, 68
commercial, vii, 1, 56, 57, 58, 67, 78
commercial bank, 78
commercial sexual exploitation of children, 57, 58, 67
communication, 96
Communist Party, 9, 20
community(s), 44, 49, 53, 58, 60, 61, 62, 74, 75, 85, 97
community service, 44, 97
compensation, 48, 55, 67, 68, 82
competition, viii, 28, 31, 36, 37, 38, 81, 88
compliance, 52, 59, 68
computer, 43
conception, 95
Concertación, 5, 6, 8, 9, 21, 22, 23
conference, 19
conflict, 61
Congress, 1, 2, 4, 5, 8, 9, 10, 11, 12, 15, 17, 21, 22, 24, 25, 28, 87, 89, 94
consensus, ix, 77
consent, 18, 58, 63
Constitution, 78, 85
constitutional amendment, 6
construction, 38, 66, 67, 68, 96
consumer markets, 6, 12
consumer protection, 11
consumers, 17, 81, 92
consumption, 13
contamination, 62
convention, 94
cooperation, vii, ix, 1, 15, 19, 20, 71, 75
coordination, 19, 66
copper, 3, 13, 14, 17, 79, 91
copyright, 85, 86
corporate governance, 88
Corporate Social Responsibility (CSR), 92
corruption, ix, 41, 46, 51, 52
cost, 34, 35, 39, 53
Costa Rica, 93
counsel, 47
counseling, 54, 55, 56
counterterrorism, 61

Coup, 22
Court of Appeals, 43
covering, 42
credentials, 43
credit market, 81, 88
credit rating, 30
creditors, 83
crimes, 43, 47, 48, 61, 92
criminal investigations, 52
criminal justice system, 42, 46, 54
crises, 19
Croatia, 93, 94
crops, 67
Cuba, 93
cultural norms, 63
currency, 58, 77, 78, 81
curricula, 73, 74
customer service, 36
Czech Republic, 93

## D

damages, 13, 48, 82
data processing, 89
database, 87
deaths, 44, 92
decentralization, 8
defendants, 47
deficiencies, 45, 85
democracy, viii, 3, 5, 8, 9, 15, 19, 41
Democrat, 5
Democratic Party, 3, 20
democratic rule, vii, 1
demonstrations, 4, 8, 9, 11, 50
Denmark, 93, 94
Department of Energy, 20
Department of Labor, 67
deposits, 37, 78, 85, 90
depreciation, 84
depth, 88
derivatives, 81
detainees, 45, 47, 48
detention, 44, 45, 46, 47, 57, 60, 61
developing countries, 87
dignity, 53
diplomatic efforts, 19
direct investment, 18
directors, 52, 91
disability, viii, 27, 30, 32, 33, 37, 38, 39, 40, 54
disaster, 19
disclosure, 52
discrimination, viii, ix, 41, 53, 56, 58, 59, 60, 61, 62, 63, 65, 71, 72, 73, 74
dissatisfaction, 2, 8, 9
dissidents, 20, 22
distribution, 9, 10, 56, 79
diversification, 30
diversity, 45, 74
domestic violence, 54, 55, 57
Dominican Republic, 93
drawing, 31
drug trafficking, 51, 52
drugs, 60, 67
due process, 82
duty free, 16

## E

earnings, 30, 36, 38, 40, 78, 84
economic activity, 95
economic assistance, 15
economic conditions, vii
economic development, 15
economic downturn, 6, 13
economic growth, ix, 2, 4, 13, 14, 38, 77
economic performance, 2
economic reform(s), 91
economic status, 60
Ecuador, 93, 94
education, 2, 3, 8, 9, 11, 12, 14, 45, 56, 59, 62, 63, 73, 74, 92, 94
education reform, 11, 12, 92
educational institutions, 11
educational settings, 57
educators, 74
Egypt, 94
El Salvador, 93
election, 3, 5, 8, 10, 12, 15, 51
electricity, 20, 64, 96, 98

e-mail, 49, 58
embassy, ix, 71, 74, 75
emergency, 56, 95
emigration, 50
employees, viii, 27, 28, 30, 32, 33, 36, 38, 39, 40, 45, 52, 57, 64, 67, 87, 93, 95
employers, viii, 27, 30, 32, 33, 35, 36, 39, 55, 64, 68
employment, 55, 56, 59, 60, 62, 66, 67, 84
energy, 2, 20, 60, 61, 79, 84
enforcement, 85
engineering, 84
entrepreneurs, 85
environment(s), 62
environmental impact, 79
environmental movement, 79
environmental protection, 8
equality, 19, 23
equity(s), 30, 81
ethnicity, 53
European Union, 12
evidence, 46, 48, 51, 55
exclusion, 60
execution, 42
executive branch, 72
expenditures, 34, 93
exploitation, 57, 58, 60, 61, 67
export control, 15
exporters, 17
exports, 14, 16, 84
exposure, 45
external shocks, 2, 13
externalities, 62

## F

Facebook, 43
families, 11
family members, 47, 54, 57
farms, 92
FDI, ix, 77, 78, 80, 84, 96, 97, 98, 99
fear, 54
Feast, 73
financial, 2, 13, 17, 20, 31, 37, 39, 52, 55, 64, 78, 81, 88, 95, 97
financial crisis, 2, 13, 17
financial institutions, 88
financial markets, 88
financial resources, 81
Finland, 93
firearms, 54
fisheries, 85
fishing, 67, 79, 84, 95
flexibility, 81, 87
food, 44
force, viii, 16, 41, 42, 43, 45, 53, 61, 79, 82, 86, 87, 88, 93, 94
foreign aid, 15, 83
foreign direct investment, ix, 12, 18, 77
foreign exchange, 78, 81
foreign investment, ix, 12, 77, 78, 79, 83, 93
foreign policy, 19
forest fire, 74
France, 25, 38, 93, 94
fraud, 52
free trade, vii, 1, 6
freedom, vii, ix, 31, 49, 50, 71, 72, 73
friendship, 62
funding, 6, 8, 9, 11, 24
funds, 13, 30, 31, 32, 37, 39, 68, 73, 79, 80, 81, 84, 88, 89, 91, 92, 97

## G

gangs, 44
GDP, 3, 11, 12, 13, 34, 89, 96
gender identity, 62
Germany, 94
global climate change, 20
Global Competitiveness Report, 23, 90
goods and services, vii, 1, 16, 96
governance, 5, 8, 14
government budget, 11
government intervention, 83
government procurement, 83
government revenues, 11, 13
governments, 6, 11, 19, 20, 52
graffiti, 74
grants, 73, 78, 82, 84
gravity, 54

Greece, 94
gross domestic product, 11, 34
growth, 13, 30, 38, 81, 88
growth rate, 38
Guatemala, 19, 94
guidance, 81
guilt, 47
guilty, 48

**H**

Haiti, 19, 25
harassment, ix, 55, 58, 71, 74
harvesting, 67
health, 14, 38, 45, 59, 63, 64, 65, 66, 68, 83, 86, 94
health care, 14, 38, 59, 63, 64
health services, 63
hemisphere, 15
high school, 73
hiring, 57, 59, 84
history, 36
HIV, 44, 63
HIV/AIDS, 44
homes, 61
Honduras, 19, 25, 94
hospitality, 65
host, 82
hotel(s), 66, 67, 97
House, 49, 65
housing, 38, 56
human, vii, viii, 6, 19, 41, 42, 45, 47, 48, 53, 61, 62
human right(s), vii, viii, 6, 41, 42, 45, 47, 48, 53, 61, 62
humanitarian organizations, 50
Hungary, 94
husband, 56

**I**

Iceland, 94
identification, 54, 65, 66, 73
identity, 63
ideology, 53
images, 39
IMF, 13, 23
immigrants, 53
imports, 17, 96
imprisonment, 54
improvements, 14, 81
incidence, 92
income, vii, viii, 2, 3, 8, 9, 14, 18, 27, 29, 30, 33, 35, 36, 38, 40, 56, 84, 87, 89, 96
income tax, 2, 18, 30, 33, 40, 84, 87, 96
independence, 3, 47
indigenous peoples, 60, 61, 62
indigenous populations, viii, 41
individual account managers, viii, 28
individual account tier, vii, viii, 27, 28, 36
individual rights, 8
individuals, 6, 29, 48, 50, 54, 55, 60, 61, 62, 85, 87
Indonesia, 94
industry(s), 35, 36, 62, 68, 79, 81, 86, 87, 88, 91
inequality, 2, 8, 11, 14, 23, 68
infection, 63
inflation, 31, 38, 58, 84
informal sector, 35, 38, 40, 68
information technology, 84
informed consent, 63
infrastructure, 13
initiation, 82
injury(s), 43, 54, 62, 65, 83
inmates, 43, 44, 45
inspections, 66
inspectors, 64, 65, 66, 68
institutions, 59, 63, 64, 66, 68, 74, 90
insurance companies, viii, 27, 30, 32, 39, 81, 89
integration, 19, 59, 81, 88
intellectual property, 17, 85
intellectual property rights, 17, 85
interfaith events, ix, 71
interference, 19
internally displaced, 50
international investment, 87
international law, 19, 79, 80, 83

International Monetary Fund, 3, 23
international standards, 87
interoperability, 15
intimidation, 61
investment(s), viii, 2, 4, 11, 13, 15, 18, 19, 28, 29, 30, 31, 34, 35, 37, 39, 77, 78, 79, 80, 81, 82, 83, 84, 88, 89, 92, 97, 98
investment capital, 80
investment incentive, 84
investors, ix, 18, 77, 78, 79, 80, 82, 83, 84, 87, 88, 89, 98
IPR, 17, 24, 85, 86
Ireland, 94
Islam, 75
issues, 2, 17, 25, 34, 45, 49, 53, 73, 74, 86
Italy, 94

## J

Japan, 17, 97, 98
Jewish Community, 58, 74
Jews, 72, 75
job training, 8
joint ventures, 78, 88
judiciary, 6, 46, 47, 48, 49
jurisdiction, 48, 59

## K

kidnapping, 43

## L

labor force, 35, 56
labor relations, 94
Latin America, 2, 12, 15, 19, 21, 22, 23, 39, 78, 89, 96
law enforcement, 46, 61, 73
laws, ix, 34, 43, 49, 51, 64, 65, 66, 68, 71, 72, 85, 93
laws and regulations, 68
lawyers, 47
lead, 17
leadership, vii, 1, 15
Lebanon, 94
legal protection, 87
legality, 46
legislation, 8, 9, 53, 61, 86, 87, 88
lending, 90
LGBT, viii, 41, 44, 45, 62
liberty, 47, 61
life expectancy, 14, 31, 34, 39
lifetime, 5, 6, 54
light, 66
liquidity, 30, 81, 88
living conditions, 9
loans, 38, 56, 80, 90
logging, 60
longevity, 31

## M

machinery, 17
magnitude, 13
majority, 3, 5, 8, 10, 11, 15, 17, 52, 64, 73, 92
Malaysia, 17, 94
malnutrition, 14
man, 56, 75
management, viii, 28, 29, 35, 36, 81, 88, 90, 91, 94
manufacturing, 66, 68, 84, 96, 97, 98
marches, 50
market access, 89
marketing, 35, 36, 86
marriage, 54, 56, 57
mass, 3, 74
material resources, 19
materials, 84
matter, ix, 77, 78, 83
measure of value, 84
media, 4, 43, 44, 45, 49, 52, 55, 57, 58, 74, 75, 85
medical, 44, 63
membership, 94
memory, 9
mergers, 35
Mexico, 17, 94, 98, 99
Miami, 25

Michelle Bachelet, viii, 2, 5, 9, 22, 24, 25, 35, 41
Middle East, 74
military, 4, 5, 6, 15, 19, 38, 40, 42, 46, 61, 64, 73, 74, 91
military courts, 46
military government, 91
military junta, 4
minimum wage, 37, 38, 67, 68
Ministry of Education, 73
minorities, 53
minors, 44, 61, 67
mission, 19, 75
Montana, 3
monthly pensions, viii, 27, 29
*Multilateral*, 94
murder, 63
music, 85
Muslims, 72

## N

national identity, 63
national interests, 82
national security, 79, 85
national strategy, 61
National Survey, 54
nationality, 53, 80
natural resources, 60, 85, 89
negotiating, 8
Netherlands, 94
New Zealand, 17, 94
NGOs, 43, 45, 55, 65, 66, 68
Nicaragua, 94
noncitizens, 52
Norway, 94
nutrition, 45

## O

OAS, 93
Obama, vii, 1, 15, 24
Obama Administration, vii, 1, 15
obstacles, 63
Organization for Economic Cooperation and Development (OECD), 14, 23, 24, 37, 38, 88, 90, 92, 93
offenders, 44, 54
officials, ix, 15, 42, 44, 45, 51, 53, 61, 71, 74, 75
oil, 17
open economy, 14
openness, 78
operations, 15, 24, 61, 78, 96
opportunities, ix, 59, 77
Organization of American States, 93
outreach, 63, 85
outsourcing, 95
Overseas Private Investment Corporation, 94
oversight, 66, 88
overtime, 67, 94
ownership, 3, 31, 32

## P

Pacific, 3, 17, 19, 24
Panama, 94, 99
Paraguay, 94
parental consent, 57
parents, 32, 57, 66, 73, 74
parole, 61
participants, 31, 32, 34, 35, 36, 50, 90
patents, 17, 81, 86
payroll, 28, 30, 32, 95
PCT, 86
peace, 15, 19, 25
peacekeepers, 19
peacekeeping, 15, 19
penalties, 51, 54, 55, 57, 64, 73
pension plans, 33, 37, 87
permission, 50, 56, 66
permit, 86, 95
perpetrators, 42, 55, 65
persons with disabilities, 59
Peru, 17, 67, 89, 94, 99
petroleum, 91
pharmaceutical, 17, 85, 86
Philippines, 94

physical abuse, 54
piracy, 85, 86, 87
plants, 20, 86
platform, 2, 11, 78, 93
playing, 88
Poland, 94
police, 19, 38, 40, 42, 43, 46, 52, 53, 54, 55, 60, 61, 62, 64, 73, 92
policy, ix, 2, 6, 11, 13, 14, 17, 18, 38, 56, 77, 92
policy makers, 17, 18
policy reform, 2, 14
political leaders, 9
political party(s), 4, 5, 9, 10, 64, 65, 93
political power, 9
political system, 49
politics, 11
polling, 59
population, 38, 44, 45, 59, 60, 72
portfolio, 80, 87, 88, 89
portfolio investment, 80
Portugal, 94
poverty, vii, viii, 2, 6, 8, 9, 14, 27, 28, 29, 33, 34, 36, 38, 60, 67
poverty line, 8
poverty prevention tier, vii, viii, 27, 28, 29, 33, 34, 36, 38
power generation, 20
preparation, 59
presidency, 5, 75
president, viii, 2, 4, 5, 6, 8, 9, 10, 11, 14, 15, 16, 17, 20, 22, 23, 24, 35, 41, 51, 74, 75, 88, 91, 94
President Obama, 15, 20, 24, 94
presidential elections, viii, 41
presidential run-off, viii, 41
presumption of innocence, 47
prevention, vii, viii, 27, 28, 29, 33, 34, 36, 38
prisoners, 44, 45, 48
prisons, 44, 45, 73
private banks, 91
private ownership, 85
private schools, 73
private sector, 37, 64, 91
producers, 17, 40, 92
profit, 11, 77, 79
project, 62, 79, 84, 85
promote innovation, 88
property rights, 17
protection, 11, 14, 17, 36, 43, 47, 50, 52, 55, 59, 79, 81, 85, 86, 88, 93
public education, 66
public enterprises, 52
public health, 11, 56
public offices, 52
public officials, 46, 52
public pension, vii, 27, 28, 29, 38
public safety, 50
public schools, 73, 74
public sector, 38, 52, 68
public service, 9, 11, 14, 93
public support, 12
publishing, 53

## Q

qualifications, 83
quality of life, 45

## R

race, 4, 53
ramp, 59
rape, 54, 55, 57, 58
rate of return, 37
ratification, 2, 25, 94
real estate, 68, 79, 85, 97
real wage, 13
recession, 17
recognition, 34
reconstruction, 8, 13
recreation, 97
redistribution, 36
reelection, 5, 10
reform(s), viii, 2, 4, 6, 8, 9, 11, 12, 19, 22, 28, 34, 35, 36, 37, 38, 39, 40, 46, 48, 51, 80, 81, 85, 87, 88, 89, 90
refugee status, 50

refugees, 50
regional cooperation, 19
regional stability, vii, 1
Registry, 67
regulations, 30, 34, 64, 65, 66, 68, 78, 81
regulatory agencies, 79
regulatory framework, 90
regulatory systems, 87
rehabilitation, 66
rehabilitation program, 66
reinsurance, 88
relief, 19
religion, 54, 73, 74
religious freedom, vii, ix, 71, 72, 73
remittances, 79, 82
renewable energy, 20, 84
repair, 67
reporters, 49
requirements, 34, 80, 83, 93
reserves, 80, 81, 90
resolution, 19, 24, 82, 87
resources, 11, 15, 20, 52, 66, 84, 89
response, 19, 52, 58, 74
restaurants, 66, 97
restitution, 61
restrictions, 49, 64, 67, 78, 79, 82
restructuring, viii, 27, 28
retail, 97
retained earnings, 84
retirement, viii, 11, 27, 28, 29, 30, 31, 32, 34, 35, 36, 39
retirement age, 28, 31, 34, 39
retribution, 54
revenue, 28
rhetoric, 75
rights, viii, 6, 9, 11, 18, 42, 43, 44, 45, 46, 47, 48, 49, 50, 53, 56, 59, 60, 61, 63, 64, 65, 66, 78, 82, 85, 86, 87, 88
risk, 30, 31, 34, 39, 81, 88, 89, 97
risk-taking, 31
Romania, 94
routes, 19, 50
royalty, 81
rules, 18, 35, 82, 83, 92
runoff, 8, 10
rural areas, 67
Russia, 94

## S

safety, 6, 54, 68, 75, 83
sanctions, 52, 54, 64
savings, vii, viii, 13, 27, 28, 29, 30, 32, 33, 36, 39, 80, 89, 90
savings account, 32, 33, 36
school, 57, 59, 66, 73, 75
schooling, 59
seafood, 17
secondary education, 11
secondary schools, 11
security(s), viii, 15, 19, 25, 41, 42, 46, 52, 61, 79, 80, 81, 84, 88, 89
securities firms, 88
security assistance, 15
security forces, viii, 41, 46, 52
segregation, 62
self-employed, viii, 28, 35, 38, 40, 89
seminars, 45, 85
Senate, 2, 5, 10, 18, 24, 25, 51, 53, 94
sentencing, 44
September 11, 4
service provider, 86
services, 17, 36, 44, 56, 59, 63, 64, 66, 84, 88, 93, 95, 96, 97
sex, 57, 58
sex offenders, 57
sexual abuse, 55, 57
sexual harassment, 55
sexual identity, 62
sexual orientation, 54, 62, 63
sexual violence, 55
shareholders, 78, 79
shortage, 87
signals, 85, 86
signs, 78
Singapore, 17
small businesses, 13, 59, 64
social programs, 14
social responsibility, 92
social security, 28, 38, 39, 40, 89

Social Security Administration, 38
social welfare, 8
societal abuses, ix, 53, 58, 71, 74
society, 4, 5, 56, 74
software, 85
solidarity, 89
South Africa, 94
South America, vii, 3, 18, 75, 90
South Korea, 94
SP, 38, 39, 40
Spain, 3, 94, 97, 98
species, 62
speech, 49
spending, 34, 45, 89
sportspersons, 67
stab wounds, 44
stability, vii, 1, 9, 15, 19, 79
state(s), 3, 4, 11, 13, 19, 29, 43, 50, 52, 53, 58, 59, 65, 72, 78, 83, 85, 90, 91, 95
state-owned enterprises, 91
statistics, 52, 68, 72, 98
stigma, 54
stimulus, 13
stock, 18, 84, 87, 88, 89
stock markets, 89
stomach, 75
storage, 97
stress, 74
structural changes, 11
structure, 36, 91
subsidy, 36
supervision, 81, 88
suppliers, 89, 95
Supreme Court, 22, 42, 61
surplus, 12, 13, 16, 38
survivors, 32
Sweden, 94
Switzerland, 94
systemic risk, 90

## T

tactics, 2, 61
target, 13
tariff, 16
tariff rates, 16
Task Force, 66
tax credits, 84
tax cuts, 13
tax data, 18
tax evasion, 11
tax incentive, 11, 33, 36, 81
tax increase, 8
taxation, 18, 30, 33, 78, 94
taxes, 8, 14, 18, 28, 78, 80, 95
tax-favored savings, viii, 28
techniques, 84
technology, 77, 84
telecommunications, 79
tensions, 9
territory, 57, 81, 85
terrorist organization, 92
tertiary education, 56
test data, 85, 86
top-down, 37
torture, 42, 44, 63
total costs, 78
tourism, 84
trade, vii, 1, 3, 4, 12, 15, 16, 17, 18, 19, 65, 91, 97
trade agreement, 3, 12, 16, 17, 18
trademarks, 87
traditions, 60
trafficking, 19, 65
training, 19, 45, 55, 56, 65, 66, 67, 68, 95
training programs, 45
transaction costs, 78
transactions, 64, 81
transfer payments, 13
transparency, 52, 61, 78, 87, 88, 93
transport, 67, 75, 84, 88, 92, 96
transportation, 17, 59, 79, 94, 96, 98
treaties, 18, 79, 94
treatment, viii, ix, 18, 41, 43, 63, 77, 79, 80, 84
trial, 47, 48, 57, 60
tuition, 11
Turkey, 94

## U

U.N. Security Council, 19
U.S. assistance, 15
U.S. Department of Commerce, 16, 24
U.S. Department of the Treasury, 25
U.S. Treasury, 25
Ukraine, 94
UNESCO, 24
unions, 64, 65, 91, 94
United, vii, 1, 3, 12, 14, 15, 16, 17, 18, 19, 20, 24, 25, 28, 37, 39, 79, 82, 86, 93, 94, 96, 97, 98, 99
United Kingdom, 94
United Nations (UN), 25, 50, 54, 61, 82, 93, 96
United States, vii, 1, 3, 12, 14, 15, 16, 17, 18, 19, 20, 24, 25, 28, 37, 39, 79, 86, 94, 97, 98, 99
universities, 85
urban, 67
urban areas, 67
Uruguay, 94, 99

## V

vandalism, ix, 58, 71, 74, 92
VAT, 95
vehicles, 17, 33
Venezuela, 94
ventilation, 44
venture capital, 81, 88
verbal slurs, ix, 58, 71, 74
victims, 6, 53, 55, 61, 65, 66, 73
Vietnam, 17, 94
violence, viii, 19, 41, 44, 46, 53, 54, 55, 56, 60, 62, 63, 73, 92
Visa Waiver Program, 15, 24
vote, 4, 5, 9, 10, 22
voters, 9, 22, 51
voting, 22, 51, 59

## W

wages, 37, 59
walking, 62, 63
Washington, 21, 22, 23, 42, 93
water, 44, 50, 62, 64, 96, 97, 98
wealth, 13, 91, 92
welfare, 4, 37
welfare state, 4
well-being, 14
White House, 15, 25
withdrawal, 30, 33
witnesses, 48
workers, viii, 27, 28, 29, 30, 33, 35, 36, 38, 39, 40, 63, 64, 65, 67, 68, 69, 89, 94, 95
workforce, 35, 37, 59, 65, 68, 94, 95
working class, 3
working conditions, 69
working hours, 94
workplace, 68
World Bank, 3, 21, 23, 38, 39, 40, 80, 87, 94
World Trade Organization (WTO), 24
worry, 17
wrongdoing, 46

## Y

young people, 67